Nelson Denny Strategy

Winning Strategies for the Nelson Denny Reading Test

Published by

ISBN-13: 978-1480151390
ISBN-10: 1480151394

Published by
Complete Test Preparation
921 Foul Bay Rd.
Victoria BC Canada V8S 4H9
Visit us on the web at http://www.test-preparation.ca
Printed in the USA

About Complete Test Preparation

The Complete Test Preparation Team has been publishing high quality study materials since 2005. Millions of students visit our websites every year, and thousands of students, teachers and parents all over the world have purchased our teaching materials, curriculum, study guides and practice tests.

Complete Test Preparation is committed to providing students with the best study materials and practice tests available on the market. Members of our team combine years of teaching experience, with experienced writers and editors, all with advanced degrees (Masters or higher).

Team Members for this publication

Editor: Brian Stocker MA
Contributor: Dr. G. A. Stocker DDS
Contributor: D. A. Stocker M. Ed.

Visit us on the web at http://www.test-preparation.ca

Contents

Getting Started with the Nelson Denny

ONGRATULATIONS! By deciding to take the Nelson Denny Reading Test, (NDRT) you have taken the first step toward a great future! Of course, there is no point in taking this important examination unless you intend to do your very best in order to earn the highest grade you possibly can. That means getting yourself organized and discovering the best approaches, methods and strategies to master the material. Yes, that will require real effort and dedication on your part but if you are willing to focus your energy and devote the study time necessary, before you know it you will be opening that letter of acceptance to the school of your dreams.

We know that taking on a new endeavour can be a little scary, and it is easy to feel unsure of where to begin. That's where we come in. This study guide is designed to help you improve your test-taking skills, show you a few tricks and increase both your competency and confidence.

The Nelson Denny Exam.

The Nelson Denny is composed of two subject areas, reading comprehension and vocabulary. Since how well you score in each of these areas will determine whether or not you get into the best school possible, it is important to be prepared. In the area of reading comprehension, examinees will be tested on their ability to comprehend reading passages, make inferences regarding those passages and draw logical conclusions. In the vocabulary section you will be tested on your word knowledge.

Test Strategy

This is a book about improving your score by using proven test strategies. This is a little different from other books such as a study guide, or a practice test. Even though we do provide lots of information to study and practice test questions, this book is about how to tackle multiple choice questions.

But do not worry - that is not all! While you are learning different strategies for answering multiple choice questions, you can also practice your skill at answering reading comprehension test questions, which are half your score on the Nelson Denny.

The other section of the Nelson Denny is vocabulary. As yo may know, the best way to improve your vocabulary is to read massive amounts of material. But if you are taking a test, that really doesn't help because it is a slow and long process. That is where the powerful vocabulary learning techniques in this book come in! We will get you up to speed fast on a huge amount of new vocabulary.

Reading Comprehension Multiple Choice Strategy

A Better Score Is Possible

WORRIED ABOUT THAT BIG EXAM COMING UP? Do you think you're just not a good test-taker, especially when it comes to standardized tests? The good news is that you're not alone. The bad news is that millions of people are left behind through objective testing, simply because they're not good test-takers. They don't know how to handle the format well or understand what's expected of them.

This is especially true of the multiple-choice test. Test-takers are given lots of support for taking essay-style tests. They're helped with skills such as grammar and spelling. However, little is offered for the multiple-choice exam. This is despite the fact that thousands of people find multiple-choice to be the most challenging kind of test. Here are some reasons that so many people have difficulties with multiple choice:

The Broad Range. Because the questions are so short and quick, a lot of ground is covered in the test. Who's to know what to study with so much material covered?

Time Limits. Most standardized tests have time limits, which adds an extra layer of pressure.

Trickery. Many test-designers think that it is too easy to guess a multiple-choice question correctly, so they intentionally make the questions tricky.

Bluffing Not Allowed. With an essay test, you can try to bluff your way through it. Not so with multiple-choice. The answer is either right or wrong.

Difficult to Write. It's not easy for a test-writer to design a good multiple-choice test. Because of this, sometimes, they make them overly difficult.

Shuffled Content. Multiple choice tests tend to throw the questions in at random, in no particular order. You could be answering a question about the 1700s and then about the 2004 Presidential election.

These challenges mean that students have to be familiar with a wider range of material than on other kinds of exams. You'll need to know specific vocabulary, rules, names, dates, etc.

There are, however, a few advantages to you, the test-taker, with a multiple-choice test. For instance, because there are more multiple-choice items on a test than there are other types, each question tends to have a lower point value. You can afford to miss a few and still be okay. Also, if you're doing a fill-in-the blank or essay test, you have to rely totally on memory to get to the answer. With a multiple-choice exam, you know that the correct answer is somewhere in the question. You just have to decide which one it is. Often, seeing the right answer will trigger your memory, and you'll recognize it instantly.

Keep in mind, though, that the test-writer knows that one of the advantages to multiple choice is the fact that the answer is on the page. This leads to many test-writers including what is called a "distracter." This is a possible answer that is designed to look like the correct answer, but which is actually wrong. We'll talk about this again later, but an example would be the question: "Who is known for posting 95 theses on a church wall?" Among the answers might be Martin Luther and Martin Luther King. Because the student vaguely remembers the name "Martin Luther" from the course materials, there's a chance that he'll select the incorrect "Martin Luther King."

WHO DOES WELL ON MULTIPLE CHOICE EXAMS?

With so many challenges working against you on the multiple-choice exam, what's the answer? Is there a way to improve your chances and your score? There is! The point of this book is not to discourage you, but to make you aware that there are strategies and tips that you can incorporate to raise your test score. Before we get into the specific strategies, let's take a general look at who does best on these types of tests.

Those who know the material. This should go without saying, but the thing that will most raise your test score will be if you know the material that's going to be covered. While the strategies we'll discuss later will help you even with questions you're unsure of, the surest thing you can do is learn the rules, dates, names, and concepts that you'll be tested on.

Those who have a calm, cool demeanor when taking a test. Panicking can cause you to forget even the information that you think you know. Confidence goes a long way toward a better mark on multiple choice.

Those who meditate or pray before the test. Don't laugh. It's a known fact that people who meditate or pray, depending on their beliefs, enter a test room more confidently and do better on the exam.

Those who operate on logic rather than instinct. Those who take a multiple-choice test based on instinct will be tempted to overlook the stated facts, and let emotion rule.

Those who have a system. Most of the book will deal with this, but you should not just guess randomly on questions you don't know. You must have a systematic strategy.

Here is a test question:

Which of the following is a helpful tip for taking a multiple-choice test?

    a. Answering "B" for all questions.

    b. Eliminate all answers that you know cannot be true.

    c. Eliminate all answers that seem like they might be true.

    d. Cheat off your neighbor.

If you answered B, you are correct. Even if you are not positive about the answer, try to get rid of as many options as possible. Think of it this way: If every item on your test has four possible answers, and if you guess on one of those four answers, you have a one in four chance of getting it right. This means that you should get one question right for every four that you have to guess on.

However, if you can get rid of two answers, then your chances improve to one in two chances. That means you will get a correct answer for every two that you guess.

So much for one of the obvious tips for improving your multiple-choice score. There are many other tips that you may or may not have considered, which will give your grade a boost. Remember, though, that none of these tips is infallible. In fact, some test-writers who know these suggestions deliberately write questions that can confound your system. Most of the time, however, you will do better on the test if you put these tips into practice.

Be prepared with all the materials you will need for the test. Bring several sheets of notebook paper, two or three sharpened pencils, an extra eraser, a high lighter, and three working pens. Why so many? Having extra materials will save you valuable time should a pencil break or a pen stop working. If you are permitted to use other aides such as a calculator, make sure the extra batteries are charged.

By familiarizing yourself with these tips, you increase your chances and who knows; you might just get a lucky break

and increase your score by a few points!

TIPS FOR READING THE INSTRUCTIONS.

Pay close attention to the sample questions. Almost all standardized tests offer sample questions, paired with their correct solutions. Go through these to make sure that you understand what they mean and how they arrived at the correct answer. Do not be afraid to ask the test supervisor for help with a sample that confuses you, or instructions that you are unsure of.

Tips for Reading the Question

We could write pages and pages of tips just on reading the test questions. Here are the ones that will help you the most.

- **Think first.** Before you look at the answer, read and think about the question. It is best to try to come up with the correct answer before you look at the options given. This way, when the test-writer tries to trick you with a close answer, you will not fall for it.

- **Make it true or false.** If a question confuses you, then look at each answer option and think of it as a "true" "false" question. Select the one that seems most likely to be "true."

- **Mark the Question.** For some reason, a lot of test-takers are afraid to mark up their test booklet. Unless you are specifically told not to mark in the booklet, you should feel free to use it to your advantage. More on this below.

- **Circle Key Words.** As you are reading the question, underline or circle key words. This helps you to focus on the most critical information needed to solve the problem. For example, if the question said, "Which of these is not a synonym for huge?" You might circle "not," "synonym" and "huge." That clears away the clutter and lets you focus on what is important. More on this below.

• **Always underline these words:** all, none, always, never, most, best, true, false and except.

• **Cross out irrelevant choices.** If you find yourself confused by lengthy questions, cross out anything that you think is irrelevant, obviously wrong, or information that you think is offered to distract you.

• **Do not try to read between the lines.** Usually, questions are written to be straightforward, with no deep, underlying meaning. The simple answer really is often the correct answer. Do not over-analyze!

GENERAL MULTIPLE CHOICE TIPS.

• **Finding Hints without Cheating** Pssst. There is a way to get hints about a question, even as you are taking the test—and it is completely legal. The key: Use the test itself to find clues about the answer. Here is how to do this. If you find that a question stumps you, read the answers. If you find one that uses the language that your teacher or textbook used, there is a good chance that this is the right answer. That is because on complex topics, teachers and books tend to always use the same or similar language.

Another point: Look out for test questions which are like previous questions. Often, you will find the same information used in more than one question.

• **Before you try eliminating wrong answers, try to solve the problem.** If you know for sure that you have answered the question correctly, then obviously there is no need to eliminate wrong choices. If you cannot solve it, then see how many choices you can eliminate. Now try solving it again and see if one of the remaining

answers comes close to your answer. Your chances of getting the answer right have now improved dramatically. Elimination is one of the most powerful strategies and we will discuss in more detail, as well as practice below.

• **Skip if you do not know.** If you simply do not know the answer and do not know how to get the answer, skip it and come back if you have time.

• **Be systematic in your guesses.** For instance, let us say you have six questions that you are able to eliminate some options, and on all of them, you have two possible answers. Pick the same answer for all six of them. If you have gotten down to two options on each of them, then chances are, you will get about three of them right.

• **Rule out answers that seem so general that they do not offer much information.** If an answer said, for example, "Columbus came to the West in the spring," it is probably not the right answer.

• **Use "all of the above" and "none of the above" to your advantage.** For "all of the above," you need not check to make sure that all of them are correct. Just check two of them. If two of the answers are correct, then this probably means they are all correct, and you can select "all." (This, of course, is not always the case, especially if there is also an option for "A and B" or "C and D."). With "all of the above" questions, you only have to find one wrong answer, and then you have eliminated two choices.

• **Let "close" answers be your guide.** The clever test-writer often includes an answer that is almost the correct one, in order to throw you off. The clever test-taker, however, can use this to his advantage. If you see two answer options that are strangely similar, then the chances are good that one of those is the correct choice. That means you can rule out the other answers—and thus improve your chances. For instance, if two choices are George Washington and George Washington Carver, among Abraham Lincoln and Thomas Edison,

there is a good chance that one of the two Washingtons is right. More on this strategy below.

Watch Out For Trick Questions

Most multiple-choice tests contain a few trick questions. A trick question is one where the test-writer intentionally makes you think that the answer is easier than it really is. Test-writers include trick questions because so many people think that they have mastered the techniques of taking a test that they need not study the material. In only a very few cases will a test have more than a handful of trick questions. Often instructors will include trick questions, where you really have to know your stuff inside-out to answer it correctly. This separates the "A" students from the "B+" students, and the "A" students from the "A+" students.

The best way to beat the trick question is to read the question carefully and break it down into parts. Then break it down into individual words. For instance, if a question asks, "When a plane crashes on the border between the United States and Canada, where are the survivors buried?" if you had looked at each word individually, you would have realized that the last word, "survivors," means that the test writer is talking about burying people who are still alive.

Before You Change That Answer ...

You are probably familiar with the concept by now: your first instinct is usually right. That is why so many people, when giving advice about tests, tell you that unless you are convinced that your first instinct was wrong, do not take a chance. It really is true that in those cases, more people change a right answer to the wrong one than change a wrong answer to a right one.

Let's take that advice a step further, though. Maybe you do not always have to leave your first answer, especially if you think there might be a reasonable chance that your second choice was right. Before you go changing the answer, though, go on and do a few questions and clear your thoughts of the problem question. After you have done a few more, go back

and start over from the beginning. Then see if the original answer is still the one that jumps out at you. If so, leave it. If your second thought now jumps out at you, then go ahead and change it. If both are equal in your mind, then leave it with your first hunch.

Answering Step-by-Step.

It might seem rather long and complicated to follow a formula for answering a multiple-choice question. After you have practiced this formula for a while, though, it will come naturally and will not take any time at all. Try to follow these steps below on each question.

Step 1. Cover up the answers while you read the question. See the material in your mind's eye and try to envision what the correct answer is before you expose the answers on the answer sheet.

Step 2. Uncover the responses.

Step 3. Eliminate. Cross out every answer that you know is ridiculous, absurd or that must clearly be wrong. Then work with the answers that remain.

Step 4. Watch for distracters. A distracter is an answer that looks very similar to the correct answer, but is put there to trip you up. If you see two answers that are strikingly similar, the chances are good that one of them is correct. For instance, if you are asked the term for the distance around a circle, and two of the responses are "periwinkle" and "perimeter," you can guess that one of these is probably correct, since the words look similar (Both start with "peri-"). Guess one of these two and your chances of correcting selecting "perimeter" are 50/50. More on this below.

Step 5. Check! If you see the answer that you saw in your mind, put a light check-mark by it and then see if any of the other choices are better. If not, mark that response as your answer.

Step 6. If all else fails, guess. If you cannot envision the correct response in your head, or figure it out by reading the passage, and if you are left totally clueless as to what the answer should be, guess.

There is a common myth that says choice "C" has a statistically greater chance of being correct. This may be true if your professor is making the test, however, most standardized tests today are generated by computer and the choices are randomized. We do not recommend choosing "C" as a strategy.

That is a quick introduction to multiple-choice to get warmed up. Next we move on to the strategies and practice test questions section. Each multiple-choice strategy is explained, followed by practice questions using the strategy. Opposite this page is a bubble sheet for answering.

MULTIPLE CHOICE STRATEGY PRACTICE QUESTIONS ANSWER SHEET.

1. Ⓐ Ⓑ Ⓒ Ⓓ   18. Ⓐ Ⓑ Ⓒ Ⓓ   35. Ⓐ Ⓑ Ⓒ Ⓓ
2. Ⓐ Ⓑ Ⓒ Ⓓ   19. Ⓐ Ⓑ Ⓒ Ⓓ   36. Ⓐ Ⓑ Ⓒ Ⓓ
3. Ⓐ Ⓑ Ⓒ Ⓓ   20. Ⓐ Ⓑ Ⓒ Ⓓ   37. Ⓐ Ⓑ Ⓒ Ⓓ
4. Ⓐ Ⓑ Ⓒ Ⓓ   21. Ⓐ Ⓑ Ⓒ Ⓓ   38. Ⓐ Ⓑ Ⓒ Ⓓ
5. Ⓐ Ⓑ Ⓒ Ⓓ   22. Ⓐ Ⓑ Ⓒ Ⓓ   39. Ⓐ Ⓑ Ⓒ Ⓓ
6. Ⓐ Ⓑ Ⓒ Ⓓ   23. Ⓐ Ⓑ Ⓒ Ⓓ   40. Ⓐ Ⓑ Ⓒ Ⓓ
7. Ⓐ Ⓑ Ⓒ Ⓓ   24. Ⓐ Ⓑ Ⓒ Ⓓ   41. Ⓐ Ⓑ Ⓒ Ⓓ
8. Ⓐ Ⓑ Ⓒ Ⓓ   25. Ⓐ Ⓑ Ⓒ Ⓓ   42. Ⓐ Ⓑ Ⓒ Ⓓ
9. Ⓐ Ⓑ Ⓒ Ⓓ   26. Ⓐ Ⓑ Ⓒ Ⓓ   43. Ⓐ Ⓑ Ⓒ Ⓓ
10. Ⓐ Ⓑ Ⓒ Ⓓ   27. Ⓐ Ⓑ Ⓒ Ⓓ   44. Ⓐ Ⓑ Ⓒ Ⓓ
11. Ⓐ Ⓑ Ⓒ Ⓓ   28. Ⓐ Ⓑ Ⓒ Ⓓ   45. Ⓐ Ⓑ Ⓒ Ⓓ
12. Ⓐ Ⓑ Ⓒ Ⓓ   29. Ⓐ Ⓑ Ⓒ Ⓓ   46. Ⓐ Ⓑ Ⓒ Ⓓ
13. Ⓐ Ⓑ Ⓒ Ⓓ   30. Ⓐ Ⓑ Ⓒ Ⓓ   47. Ⓐ Ⓑ Ⓒ Ⓓ
14. Ⓐ Ⓑ Ⓒ Ⓓ   31. Ⓐ Ⓑ Ⓒ Ⓓ   48. Ⓐ Ⓑ Ⓒ Ⓓ
15. Ⓐ Ⓑ Ⓒ Ⓓ   32. Ⓐ Ⓑ Ⓒ Ⓓ   49. Ⓐ Ⓑ Ⓒ Ⓓ
16. Ⓐ Ⓑ Ⓒ Ⓓ   33. Ⓐ Ⓑ Ⓒ Ⓓ   50. Ⓐ Ⓑ Ⓒ Ⓓ
17. Ⓐ Ⓑ Ⓒ Ⓓ   34. Ⓐ Ⓑ Ⓒ Ⓓ

The following are detailed strategies for answering multiple choice questions with practice questions for each strategy.

Answers appear following this section with a detailed explanation and discussion on each strategy and question, plus tips and analysis.

STRATEGY 1 - LOCATE KEYWORDS.

For every question, figure out exactly what the question is asking by locating key words that are in the question.

Directions: Read the passage below and answer the questions using this strategy.

Free range is a method of farming husbandry where the animals are allowed to roam freely instead of being enclosed in a pen. The term is used in two senses that do not overlap completely: as a farmer-centric description of husbandry methods, and as a consumer-centric description of them. Farmers practice free range to achieve free-range or humane certification (and thus capture high prices), to reduce feed costs, to improve the happiness and liveliness of their animals, to produce a higher-quality product, and as a method of raising multiple crops on the same land. [1]

1. The free-range method of farming

    a. Uses a minimum amount of fencing to give animals more room

    b. Can refer to two different things

    c. Is always a very humane method

    d. Only allows for one crop at a time

2. Free range farming is practiced

    a. To obtain free-range certification

    b. To lower the cost of feeding animals

    c. To produce higher quality product

    d. All of the above

3. Free range farming husbandry:

   a. Can mean either farmer described or consumer described methods

   b. Is becoming much more popular in many areas

   c. Has many limits and causes prices to go down

   d. Is only done to make the animals happier and healthier

4. Free range certification is most important to farmers because:

   a. Free-range livestock are less expensive to feed

   b. The price of the product is higher

   c. Both 1 and 2

   d. The animals are kept in smaller enclosures, so more can be produced

STRATEGY 2 - WATCH NEGATIVES.

For every question, no matter what type, look for words that are associated with negatives. These can include always, all, most, never, not, and others that will completely change what is being asked.

Directions: Read the passage below and answer the questions using this strategy.

Male grizzly bears can weight more than 1,000 pounds, but more typically weigh 400 pounds to 770 pounds. The females are on average 38% smaller, at about 250–350 pounds, an example of sexual dimorphism. On average, grizzly bears stand about 1 meter (3.3 ft.) at the shoulder when on all fours and 2 meters (6.6 ft.) on their hind legs, but males often stand 2.44 meters (8 ft.) or more on their hind legs. On average, grizzly bears from the Yukon River area are about 20% smaller than typical grizzlies.[2]

5. Sexual dimorphism does not mean

a. Male grizzly bears are the same size as the female of the species

b. All grizzly bears look the same and are the same size

c. Grizzly bears can be quite large, and weigh more than half a ton

d. All of the above

6. The size of a full-grown grizzly bear is never

a. More than 500 pounds

b. Dependent on what sex the bear is

c. Determined simply by diet

d. More than 6 feet tall

7. Grizzly bears from the area of the Yukon River do not

a. Get as big as most other grizzly bears do

b. Get the rich and varied food supply needed

c. Need the same nutrients as other grizzly bears

d. Get less than 7 feet tall, and weigh close to half of a ton

STRATEGY 3 – READ THE STEM COMPLETELY.

For every question, no matter what type, read the information in the stem and then try to determine the correct answer before you look at the different answers.

Directions: Read the passage below and answer the questions using this strategy.

Formerly, taxonomists listed brown and grizzly bears as separate species. Technically, brown and grizzly bears are classified as the same species, Ursus Arctos. The term "brown bear" is commonly used to refer to the members of this species found in coastal areas where salmon is the primary food source. Brown bears found inland and in northern habitats

are often called "grizzlies." Brown bears on Kodiak Island are classified as a distinct subspecies from those on the mainland because they are genetically and physically isolated. The shape of their skulls also differs slightly. [3]

8. Grizzly bears, brown bears, and kodiak bears are all

  a. Arctas Ursinas

  b. Ursus Arctos

  c. Arctos Ursina

  d. Ursula Arctic

9. Kodiak brown bears are classified as a different subspecies because

  a. They are much larger than other brown bears

  b. Their diet is radically different from that of other brown bears

  c. They are not true brown bears but instead a mixture of bear species

  d. Of their genetics and head shape, as well as the physical isolation

10. The term grizzlies, when referring to the brown bear, is used mainly

  a. In eastern areas where the bear grows large

  b. Only in snowy areas where there are low year round temperatures

  c. In the northern and central areas

  d. In areas where the bear has a silver appearance

11. The term brown bear is normally used

  a. When one of the main food sources is salmon

  b. When the bear is small

  c. When the bear is found inland

  d. When the bear has a light brown coat and is very large

STRATEGY 4 - READ ALL THE CHOICES FIRST.

For every question, no matter what type, make sure to read every option before determining which option is the right one.

Directions: Read the passage below and answer the questions using this strategy.

Jim Martell, a hunter from Idaho, reportedly found and shot a grizzly-polar bear hybrid near Sachs Harbor on Banks Island, Northwest Territories, Canada, on April 16, 2006. Martell had been hunting for polar bears with an official license and a guide, at a cost of $50,000, and killed the animal believing it to be a normal polar bear. Officials took interest in the creature after noticing that it had thick, creamy white fur, typical of polar bears, as well as long claws; a humped back; a shallow face; and brown patches around its eyes, nose, and back, as well as patches on one foot, which are all traits of grizzly bears. If the bear had been adjudicated to be a grizzly, he would have faced a possible CAN$1,000 fine and up to a year in jail. A DNA test conducted by the Wildlife Genetics International in British Columbia confirmed that it was a hybrid, with the mother a polar bear and the father a grizzly. It is the first documented case in the wild, though it was known that this hybrid was biologically possible and other hybrids have been bred in zoos in the past.[3]

12. Which grizzly bear features did the hybrid bear have?

    a. Brown patches in certain areas

    b. Long claws

    c. A shallow face

    d. All of the above

13. The hybrid bear was the result of

    a. A male brown bear and a female grizzly

    b. A female brown bear and a male grizzly bear

    c. A female polar bear and a male grizzly bear

    d. A male polar bear and a female grizzly

 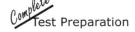

14. The hybrid bear tested in this case was

a. The first case ever known where two different bear species mated successfully

b. Genetically flawed and prone to many diseases and conditions

c. A fluke, and a mistake of nature which has never happened before

d. The first proof of a wild bear hybrid species outside of zoos

15. Modern science

a. Has proven that the cubs from two different species will not survive in almost every case

b. Has known for some time that these hybrid bears were possible

c. Completely understands how bear hybrids occur and why this happens in nature

d. Has studied hundreds of bear hybrids in an attempt to learn more

STRATEGY 5 - ELIMINATION.

For every question, no matter what type, eliminating obviously incorrect answers narrows the possible choices. Elimination is probably the most powerful strategy for answering multiple choice.

Directions: Read the passage below and answer the questions using this strategy.

The male peafowl, or peacock, has long been known and valued for its brilliant tail feathers. The bright spots on it are known as "eyes," and inspired the Greek myth that Hera placed the hundred eyes of the slain giant Argus on the tail of her favorite bird. Indian Peafowl are iridescent blue-green or blue in the head, neck and breast. The back, or scapular, feathers are vermiculated in black and white, while the primaries are orange-chestnut. The so-called "tail" of the peacock, also termed the "train," is not the tail quill feathers but highly elongated upper tail feathers. It is mostly bronze-green, with a series of eyes that are best seen when the train is fanned. The actual tail feathers are short and grey-colored and can be seen from behind when a peacock's train is fanned in a courtship display. During the molting season, the males shed their stunning train feathers and reveal the unassuming grey-colored tail which is normally hidden from view beneath the train. The female peacock is duller in comparison. It is mostly brown, with pale under-parts and some green iridescence in the neck, and lacks the long upper tail feathers of the male. [4]

16. The long colorful tail feathers of the peacock

> a. Are only present in the male of the species
>
> b. Are used by both sexes to warn off predators
>
> c. Are normally red and blue in color
>
> d. Are only present for a very short time each year

17. The differences between the male and female peacock are

> a. Size and weight
>
> b. Coloring and tail feather length
>
> c. The female does not ever leave the nest
>
> d. The male sits on and hatches the eggs

18. The term peacock actually refers to

> a. Both sexes from the pheasant family
>
> b. The eyes on the tail feathers of the bird
>
> c. The male bird of the peafowl species
>
> d. The female bird of the peafowl species

19. The gray tail feathers on the male peacock can be seen

    a. When the bird is startled

    b. Only when the bird is searching for food

    c. When the peacock lowers the tail feathers to the ground

    d. During molting

STRATEGY 6 - OPPOSITES.

For every question, no matter what type, look at answers that are opposites. When two answers are opposites, the odds increase that one of them is the correct answer.

Directions: Read the passage below and answer the questions using this strategy.

Smallpox is an infectious disease unique to humans, caused by either of two virus variants, the Variola Major or Variola Minor. The disease is also known by the Latin names Variola or Variola vera, which is a derivative of the Latin varius, meaning spotted.

Smallpox localizes in small blood vessels of the skin and in the mouth and throat. In the skin, this results in a characteristic rash, and later, blisters. Variola Major produces a more serious disease and has an overall mortality rate of 30–35%. Variola Minor causes a milder form of disease (also known as alastrim, cottonpox, milkpox, whitepox, and Cuban itch) which kills about 1% of its victims. Long-term complications of Variola major infection include characteristic scars, commonly on the face, which occur in 65–85% of survivors. Blindness and limb deformities due to arthritis and osteomyelitis are less common complications, seen in about 2–5% of cases.
[5]

20. Smallpox

a. Effects all mammals, including humans

b. Is caused by a bacteria from contact with dead flesh

c. Was called the great pox during the fifteenth century

d. Only affects humans, although other species can carry and transmit the virus

21. Smallpox caused by Variola major has a

a. Thirty to thirty five percent survival rate

b. Sixty percent mortality rate

c. Thirty to thirty five percent mortality rate

d. Sixty percent survival rate

22. Smallpox caused by Variola minor is

a. Much more severe, with a greater number of pox and more scarring

b. Much less severe, with fewer pox and less scarring

c. Characterized because there are no pox

d. So minor that no treatment or medical attention is needed

23. Smallpox can be fatal

a. In between thirty and thirty five percent of those who catch the virus, depending on the type

b. In between thirty and sixty five percent of those who catch the virus, depending on the type

c. When no medical treatment is available

d. Only in developing countries where medical care is poor

STRATEGY 7 - LOOK FOR DIFFERENCES

For every question, no matter what type, look at the two choices that seem to be correct and then examine the differences between the two. Refer to the stem to determine the

best answer.

Directions: Read the passage below and answer the questions using this strategy.

Lightning is an atmospheric discharge of electricity accompanied by thunder, which typically occurs during thunderstorms, and sometimes during volcanic eruptions or dust storms. Atmospheric electrical discharges, or bolts of lightning, can travel at speeds of 130,000 mph, and reach temperatures approaching 54,000° F, hot enough to fuse silica sand into glass channels known as fulgurites that are normally hollow and can extend some distance into the ground. There are some 16 million lightning storms in the world every year.

The irrational fear of lightning and thunder is astraphobia.

Lightning can also occur within the ash clouds of volcanic eruptions, or can be caused by violent forest fires which generate sufficient dust to create a static charge.

How lightning initially forms is still a matter of debate: Scientists have studied root causes ranging from atmospheric perturbations (wind, humidity, friction, and atmospheric pressure) to the impact of solar wind and accumulation of charged solar particles. Ice inside a cloud is thought to be a key element in lightning development, and may cause a forcible separation of positive and negative charges within the cloud, thus assisting in the formation of lightning.[6]

24. Astraphobia is

    a. Fear of thunder

    b. Fear of thunder and lightning

    c. Fear of lightning

    d. None of the above

25. Lightning occurs

a. Only in thunderstorms

b. In thunderstorms and dust storms

c. In thunderstorms, volcanic eruptions and dust storms

d. In the upper atmosphere

26. Fulgurites are

a. Made of silica

b. Made of glass

c. Made of silica turned in to glass

d. Made of silica and glass

STRATEGY 8 – CONTEXT CLUES.

Looked at the sentences, and the context to determine the best option. In some cases, the answer to the question may be located right in the passage or question.

Directions: Read the passage below and answer the questions using this strategy.

Venus is one of the four solar terrestrial planets, meaning that, like the Earth, it is a rocky body. In size and mass, it is very similar to the Earth, and is often described as its "sister," or Earth's twin. The diameter of Venus is only 650 km. less than the Earth's, and its mass is 81.5% of the Earth's. However, conditions on the Venusian surface differ radically from those on Earth, due to its dense carbon dioxide atmosphere. The mass of the atmosphere of Venus is 96.5% carbon dioxide, with most of the remaining 3.5% nitrogen.

Venus is the second-closest planet to the Sun, orbiting every 224.7 Earth days. The planet is named after Venus, the Roman goddess of love and beauty. After the Moon, it is the brightest natural object in the night sky, reaching an apparent magnitude of −4.6. Because Venus is an inferior planet from Earth, it never appears to venture far from the Sun: its elongation reaches a maximum of 47.8°. Venus reaches its maximum brightness shortly before sunrise or shortly after sunset, and is often called the Morning Star or the Evening Star. [1]

27. Apparent magnitude is

a. A measure of darkness

b. A measure of brightness

c. The distance from the moon

d. The distance from the earth

28. The elongation of a planet is

a. The angular distance from the sun, as seen from earth.

b. The distance from the sun

c. The distance form the earth

d. None of the above

29. Terrestrial planets are

a. Made of rock

b. Have people on them

c. The earth and no others

d. The same size as Earth

30. How many planets orbit the sun in less than 224.7 days?

a. 1 planet

b. Only Venus

c. 2 planets

d. 3 planets

STRATEGY 9 - TRY EVERY OPTION.

For definition questions, try out all of the options - one option will fit better than the rest. As you go through the options, use Strategy 5 - Elimination to eliminate obviously incorrect choices as you go.

Directions: Read the passage below and answer the questions using this strategy.

On Earth, common weather phenomena include wind, cloud, rain, snow, fog and dust storms. Less common events include natural disasters such as tornadoes, hurricanes, typhoons and ice storms. Almost all weather phenomena occurs in the troposphere (the lower part of the atmosphere). Weather does occur in the stratosphere and can affect weather lower down in the troposphere, but the exact mechanisms are poorly understood.

Weather occurs primarily due to different temperature and moisture densities. The strong temperature contrast between polar and tropical air gives rise to the jet stream. Weather systems in the mid-latitudes, such as extra tropical cyclones, are caused by instabilities of the jet stream flow. Weather systems in the tropics, such as monsoons or thunderstorms, are caused by different processes.

Because the Earth's axis is tilted relative to its orbital plane, sunlight is incident at different angles at different times of the year. In June the Northern Hemisphere is tilted towards the sun, so at any given Northern Hemisphere latitude, sunlight is more direct than in December. This effect causes seasons. Over thousands to hundreds of thousands of years, changes in Earth's orbital parameters affect the amount and distribution of solar energy received by the Earth and influence long-term climate. [8]

31. The troposphere is

    a. The highest strata of the atmosphere

    b. The lowest strata of the atmosphere

    c. The middle level of the atmosphere

    d. Not part of the atmosphere

32. Monsoons are

    a. Caused by instabilities in the jet stream

    b. Caused by processes other than instabilities in the jet stream

    c. Part of the jet stream

    d. Cause the jet stream

33. Extra-tropical cyclones occur

    a. In the tropics

    b. In temperate zones

    c. In the gulf stream

    d. In mid-latitudes

34. Tilted means:

    a. Slanted

    b. Rotating

    c. Connected to

    d. Bent

STRATEGY 10 - WORK FOR IT.

For questions about supporting details, work is the key. Review the passage to locate the right option. Never forget the choices that you are given are designed to confuse, and they may *seem* reasonable answers to the question. However, if they are not mentioned in the text, they are "red herring" answers.

The best answer is the exact answer mentioned in the text.

Directions: Read the passage below and answer the questions using this strategy.

Ebola is the common term for a group of viruses belonging to genus Ebola virus (EBOV), which is a part of the family Filoviridae, and for the disease that they cause, Ebola hemorrhagic fever. The virus is named after the Ebola River, where the first recognized outbreak of Ebola hemorrhagic fever occurred. The viruses are characterized by long filaments, and have a shape similar to that of the Marburg virus, also in the family Filoviridae, and possessing similar disease symptoms. There are a number of species within the Ebola virus genus, which in turn have a number of specific strains or serotypes. The Zaire virus is the type species, which is also the first discovered and the most lethal. Ebola is transmitted primarily through bodily fluids and to a limited extent through skin. The virus interferes with the endothelial cells lining the interior surface of blood vessels and platelet cells. As the blood vessel walls become damaged and the platelets are unable to coagulate, patients succumb to hypovolemic shock. Ebola first emerged in 1976 in Zaire. It remained largely obscure until 1989 with the outbreak in Reston, Virginia.[9]

35. The Ebola virus received this name because of

    a. The doctor who first discovered the virus

    b. The cure that is used to treat those infected

    c. The river where the disease was first encountered

    d. What the virus does to the body

36. Viruses in the Ebola genus are recognizable

    a. Because of their hooked shape

    b. Because of their long filaments

    c. Due to their oblong heads

    d. Because of their unique color

37. One of the most common causes of death from the Ebola family of viruses is

    a. Hypovolemic shock due to blood vessel damage

    b. Bleeding of the brain that cannot be stopped

    c. A heart attack from blood loss and lack of fluids

    d. A high fever that cannot be lowered

 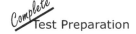

38. The most deadly strain of the Ebola virus family is the

    a. The Reston strain

    b. The Ivory Coast strain

    c. The Zaire strain

    d. The Sudan strain

STRATEGY 11 - LOOK AT THE BIG PICTURE.

Details can be tricky when dealing with main idea and summary questions, but do not let the details distract you. Look at the big picture instead of the smaller parts to determine the right answer.

Directions: Read the passage below and answer the questions using this strategy.

As of late 2005, three fruit bat species have been identified as carrying the Ebola virus but not showing disease symptoms. They are now believed to be a natural host species, or reservoir, of the virus. Plants, arthropods, and birds have also been considered as reservoirs; however, bats are considered the most likely candidate. Bats were known to reside in the cotton factory where the first outbreaks in 1976 and 1979 occurred, and they have also been implicated in Marburg infections in 1975 and 1980. Of 24 plant species and 19 vertebrate species experimentally inoculated with Ebola virus, only bats became infected. The absence of clinical signs in these bats is characteristic of a reservoir species. In 2002-03, a survey of 1,030 animals from Gabon and the Republic of the Congo including 679 bats found Ebolavirus RNA in 13 fruit bats (Hypsignathus monstrosus, Epomops franquetti and Myonycteris torquata). Bats are also known to be the reservoirs for a number of related viruses including Nipah virus, Hendra virus and Lyssaviruses.[2]

39. The species most suspected as a potential Ebola virus reservoir is

    a. Birds

    b. Insects

    c. Plants

    d. Bats

40. Most plant and animal species

    a. Can carry the Ebola virus but not become infected

    b. Can not carry and transmit the Ebola virus

    c. Are responsible for new cases of Ebola viruses

    d. Can be infected with one of the Ebola viruses

41. Bats are known for

    a. Being carriers of many different viruses, including Ebola

    b. Transmitting the Ebola virus through a scratch

    c. Being susceptible to the virus and becoming infected

    d. Transmitting the Ebola virus through infected droppings

STRATEGY 12 - BEST POSSIBLE ANSWER.

Try to determine the best possible answer according to the information given in the passage. Do not be distracted by answers that seem correct or are mostly correct.

  Directions: Read the passage below and answer the questions using this strategy.

In the early stages, Ebola may not be highly contagious. Contact with someone in early stages may not even transmit the disease. As the illness progresses, bodily fluids represent an extreme biohazard. Due to lack of proper equipment and hygienic practices, large-scale epidemics occur mostly in poor, isolated areas without modern hospitals or well-edu-

cated medical staff. Many areas where the infectious reservoir exists have just these characteristics. In such environments, all that can be done is immediately cease all needle sharing or use without adequate sterilization procedures, to isolate patients, and to observe strict barrier nursing procedures with the use of a medical rated disposable face mask, gloves, goggles, and a gown at all times. This should be strictly enforced for all medical personnel and visitors. [10]

42. Ebola is highly contagious

a. Only when blood is present

b. Only in the first stages before hemorrhaging occurs

c. At all stages of the illness from incubation to recovery

d. Only in the later stages when the virus is very numerous

43. Exposure to the Ebola virus means

a. A death sentence for most patients

b. Isolation for the patient, and proper precautions for all medical personnel to contain the virus

c. The virus will spread rapidly and there is no treatment available

d. A full recovery usually, with very few symptoms

44. Ebola outbreaks commonly occur

a. Because sterilization and containment procedures are not followed or available

b. Due to infected animals in the area

c. Because of rat droppings in homes

d. Because of a contaminated water supply

45. Ebola is

a. More common in advanced nations where treatment makes the disease minor

b. More common in third world and developing countries

c. Fatal in more than ninety-five percent of the cases

d. Highly contagious during the incubation period

Answers to Sample Multiple Choice Strategy Questions

Strategy 1 - Keywords in the question tells what the question is asking

1. B
The question asks about the free range *method* of farming. Here method refers to *type* of farming. "Method" here is the keyword and can be marked or underlined.

2. D
The Question is, "Free-range farming is *practiced* ..." The keyword here is "practiced." Looking at the choices, which all start with "to," it is clear the answer will be about *why* free range ... Also notice that one of the choices is "All of the above," which in this case is the correct answer. However, when "All of the above" is an option, this is a potential Elimination strategy. All you have to do is find one option that is incorrect and you can use Strategy 5 - Elimination to eliminate two choices and increase your odds from one in four, to one in two.

3. A
The question is, "Free range farming husbandry ..." From the question, and the *lack* of keywords, together with the choices presented, the answer will be a definition free range farming husbandry.

4. C
The question is, "Free-range certification is *most important* to farmers because ... " The keywords here are "most important." Be careful to choose the best possible answer.

Strategy 2 - Negatives

These four questions all have negatives: does not mean, is never, do not, and is not. These questions exclude possibilities, so if you see any choices that are true, you can eliminate them right away.

5. D

The question asks what sexual dimorphism does *not* mean. Circle the word "not" and keep it firmly in mind. Next, what is sexual dimorphism. Reading the text quickly, sexual dimorphism is not defined explicitly but related to the female bears being smaller than the males. Probably there are other aspects, but this general definition is all that is needed to answer the question.

First, notice that "All of the above" is Choice D. In addition the question is a negative. So in order for Choice D to be correct, Choices A, B and C must be *in*correct. This narrows down your options. If any of Choices A, B or C are correct, then you can eliminate that choice as well as Choice D.

Either all of the choices are *in*correct, in which case, Choice D, "All of the above" is correct.

Choice A, male and females are the same size is incorrect. Choice B, all grizzly bears look the same and are the same size, is incorrect.
Choice C, grizzly bears (plural so *all* grizzly bears) can be large and weigh more than half a ton. This is incorrect since while all grizzly bears are large, female bears weight less than half a ton.

All three choices are incorrect so Choice D is the correct answer, All of the above are incorrect.

6. A

First, circle or underline never to show this is a negative question. Now look at the options to find an option that is not true.

Choice A is true as male bears are 1,000 pounds. Place a mark beside this one. It may be tempting to select this option as your answer, but it is important to look at all choices before making a final decision.

Choice B is not true - size does not depend on the sex.
Choice C is not true - size does not depend on diet.
Choice D is not true - males often stand 8 feet.

So Choice A is correct.

7. A

First circle "do not" to mark this as a negative question.

Choice A is correct, Yukon River grizzly bears do not get as big as other grizzlies, so put a mark beside it for later consideration. Examine the other choices before making a final decision.

Choice B is not mentioned in the text, and can be eliminated.

Choice C is not mentioned in the text and can be eliminated.

Choice D is true, but this is a negative question so it is false.

Some of the above choices may be true from a common sense point of view, but if they aren't mentioned specifically in the passage, they can be eliminated.

Choice A is correct.

Strategies 3 - Read the stem completely.

Read the question, and then look for the answer in the text before reading the choices. Reading the choices first will confuse, just as it is meant to do! Do not fall into this trap!

8. B

The choices here are very confusing and are meant to be! Four variations on the latin species name, Ursus Arctos are given, so the question is what version of this latin name is correct, which gives a very straight-forward strategy to solving. Since the name is latin, it is going to stand out in the text. Take the first option, "Arctas Ursinas," and scan the text for something that looks like that. At the end of the second sentence is "Ursus Arctos," which is very close. Next confirm what this sentence refers to, which gives the correct answer, Choice B.

9. D

This question asks why Kodiak brown bears are a different subspecies, and the options are designed to confuse a careless, stressed test-taker. Scan the text for "Kodiak," which appears in the second to last sentence, and answers the question.

10. C

This question asks about the relationship between brown bears and grizzly bears. If you are not careful you will be confused by the choices.

11. A

Read the question, then read the text before trying to answer and avoid confusion.

Strategy 4 - Read every choice before deciding.

In Strategy 3, we learned to find the correct answer in the text before reading the choices. OK, now you have read the text and have the right answer. The next thing is Strategy 4 - Read *all* of the choices. Once you have read all of the choices, select the correct choice.

12. D

First, notice that "All of the above" is a choice. So if you find one option that is incorrect, you can eliminate that option and option D, "All of the above." Reading the question first, (Strategy #3) then looking in the text, and then reading all of the choices before answering, you can see that choices A, B and C are all correct, so choice D, All of the Above, is the correct choice.
If you had not read all the choices first, then you might be tempted to impulsively choose A, B, or C as the answer.

13. C

Looking at the choices, they are designed to confuse with different choices and combinations. Recognizing this, it is therefore important to be extra careful in making your choice. If you are stressed, in a hurry, or not paying attention, you will probably get this question wrong by making an impulsive choice and not reading through all the choices before making a selection.

Referring to the text, you will find the sentence, "... it was a hybrid, with the mother a polar bear and the father a grizzly," which answers the question.

14. D

Reading through all of the choices, B and C can be eliminated right away as they are not referred to in the text. They might appear as good answers but they are not from the passage.

Looking at A and D, the issue is if this has happened before, or has it happened only in zoos. Referring to the text, the last sentence tells us the answer, "It is the first documented case in the wild, though it was known that this hybrid was biologically possible and other hybrids have been bred in zoos in the past."

15. B
Reading through the four choices, the question concerns, what does science know? Does it happen all the time? Completely understood? They do survive? Is it possible? Look in the text for how much is known. The last sentence, "It is the first documented case in the wild, though it was known that this hybrid was biologically possible" gives the answer.

Strategy 5 - Elimination.

For every question, no matter what type, eliminating obviously incorrect answers narrows the possible choices. Elimination is probably the most powerful strategy for answering multiple choice.

16. A
Using this strategy the choices can be narrowed down to A and D. I have never seen a peacock with red in their tail, so C can *probably* be eliminated, but check back. Most birds and many animals have a pattern where the male is colorful and the female less colorful. Choice B can be eliminated as it refers to "both sexes" having colorful tails. Choice D is a good candidate as the text refers to molting season, however, the text does not say how long this is, so there is some doubt. This makes A the best choice as it is referred to directly in the text.

17. B
Choice D can be eliminated right away, as it is rare for a male bird to sit on eggs.

Skimming the passage, choices A and C can be eliminated, as they are not mentioned directly in the text, leaving only D.

18. C

Choices A and D can be eliminated right away, since "cock" always refers to a male bird. Referring to the text, "The male peafowl, or peacock, has long been ..." making C the best choice.

19. D

Choices A and B can be eliminated either right away or with a quick check of the passage, since they are not mentioned. Choice C is suspicious since the grey feathers are under the tail feathers, so it is difficult to see how they could be visible when the tail feathers are lowered.

Strategy 6 - Opposites

If there are opposites, one of them is generally the correct answer. If it helps, make a table that lays out the different options and the correct option will become clear.

20. D

Notice that A and D are opposites. Referring to the text, "Smallpox is an infectious disease unique to humans ..." eliminates choice A.

21. C

Notice that all of the choices are opposites. 30 - 35% mortality, or survival rate, or 60%. Therefore, the task is to review the text, looking for 30% or 60%, survival or mortality, stay clear, and do not get confused. Sometimes making notes or a table can help to clarify.

The question is asking about percent, so it is easy and fast to skim the passage for a percent sign.

The first percent sign is in the second paragraph, 30 - 35%. Write this in the margin. Next, see what this percent refers to, which is the mortality rate. Write "mortality" next to 30 - 35%. Now, working backwards, see what the 30 - 35% mortality rate refers to. At the beginning of that sentence, is Variola Major. Now we have a clear understanding of what the passage is saying, which we have retrieved quickly and easily, and now hopefully we will not get confused by the different choices.

Choice A and B can be eliminated right away. Choice C looks correct. Check Choice D quickly, and confirm that it is incorrect. Choice C is the correct answer.

22. B

Choices A and B are opposites. Is Variola Minor more or less severe, with more or fewer pox, and more or less scarring? The other two choices, "no pox" and "no treatment" can be eliminated quickly. Either choice A or B are going to be wrong, which is confirmed by the text.

Make a quick table like this:

Major - more serious - scars, blindness
Minor - milder

The passage does not mention scarring from Variola minor, but we can infer that it is milder. Looking at the options, Choice A is clearly talking about Variola major, and we can infer that Choice B is talking about Variola minor and is the correct answer. We can confirm our inference from the text.

23. A

Choices A and B are not exactly opposite, but very close and designed to confuse if you do not read them properly. How many people die from the virus? Between 30 and 35%? Or between 35 and 60%? Scan the text with these numbers in mind.

This question is asking about a percent figures, so quickly scan the passage for a percent sign, which first appears in the second paragraph. Working back from there confirm that the percent figures is related to mortality, which it is.

Strategy 7 - Look for Differences.

Look at two choices that appear to be correct and examine them carefully.

24. B

Choices A, B and C are very similar and designed to confuse and distract someone who does not look carefully at the text. What is astraphobia exactly? This is a definition question for an unusual word, astraphobia. Scan the text for "astraphobia." Choice B is correct.

25. C
Choices A, B and C are similar and designed to confuse, or tempt a stressed or careless test-taker into making a quick and incorrect choice. Checking the passage, in the first paragraph, lightning occurs in thunderstorms, volcanic eruptions and in dust storms, so choice C is correct.

26. C
All four answers are similar and designed to confuse. Seeing how similar the choices are, it is very important to be clear on the exact definition. This is a definition question, so scan the text quickly for the word "fulgurites." From the first paragraph, fulgurites are formed when lightning is ".. hot enough to fuse silica sand into glass channels ..." so the correct answer, and the option that answers the question the best, is choice C, "Made of silica turned into glass."

Strategy 8 - Context clues

Look at the sentences, and the context to determine the best option. In some cases, the answer to the question may be located right in the passage or question.

27. B
You do not have to know the exact meaning - just enough to answer the question. The phrase is used in the passage, "After the Moon, it is the brightest natural object in the night sky, reaching an apparent magnitude of −4.6" where Venus is compared to the brightness of the moon, so the apparent magnitude must have something to do with brightness, which is enough information to answer the question. Notice also, how the choices are opposites. Choice A and B are opposites as are choices C and D.

28. A
The exact meaning is not necessary, you only need only enough information to answer the question. The passage is, "Because Venus is an inferior planet from Earth, it never appears to venture far from the Sun: its elongation reaches a maximum of 47.8°." Elongation in this sentence is some-

 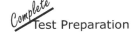

thing connected with distance from the sun, but also something to do with Earth. Choices C and D can be eliminated right away. Choice A is the most likely correct because it mentions, "as seen from earth."

29. A
Terrestrial has many similar meanings, but choice A is the best. From the passage, "Venus is one of the four solar terrestrial planets, meaning that, like the Earth, it is a rocky body." Choice C can be eliminated right away. No mention is made of size or people, so choices C and D are also incorrect.

Note that Choice B is a grammatical error and can be eliminated right away. The question is, "Terrestrial planets are," and Choice B is, "Have people on them."

This is a great strategy, looking for grammatical errors and eliminating, and what you might expect to see on a test that a professor has made themselves. However, most standardized tests are generated by computer, and proofed by many different people who have considerable expertise in correcting this type of easy question. Keep this in mind, but don't expect to see this type of thing on a standardized test.

30. A
All of the choices are similar and designed to confuse. Venus is the second closest planet to the sun so there must be one planet that is closer. Planets closer to the sun will rotate the sun faster, so the answer must be choice A.

Strategy 9 - Try out every option for word meaning questions.

For definition questions, try out all of the options - one option will fit better than the rest. As you go through the options, use Strategy 5 - Elimination to eliminate obviously incorrect choices as you go.

31. B
The answer is taken directly from the passage. Notice that choices A and B are opposites, so one of them will be incorrect. Look in the text carefully for the exact definition. If you are uncertain, make a table in the margin.

32. B

The choices are designed to confuse. The sentences talking about the jet stream and monsoons are next to each other. Trying each definition and comparing to the text, only choice B fits. If you are uncertain, make a table in the margin.

33. B

Trying each definition choice, Choice B is the only answer that makes sense referring to the text. The choices are designed to confuse, making it very important that you be extra careful to find the exact definition from the text.

34. A

The passage from the text is, "Because the Earth's axis is tilted relative to its orbital plane, sunlight is incident at different angles at different times of the year." Substituting all of the choices given into this sentence, slanted, choice 1, is the only sensible answer. Here is what substitutions look like:

> a. In June the Northern Hemisphere is *slanted* towards the sun...
>
> b. In June the Northern Hemisphere is *rotating* towards the sun...
>
> c. In June the Northern Hemisphere is *connected to* towards the sun...
>
> d. In June the Northern Hemisphere is *bent* towards the sun...

Choice A is the only one that makes sense.

Strategy 10 - You have to work for it! Check carefully for supporting details.

All of these answers can be found by carefully reading the text. The questions paraphrase the text found in the passage.

35. C

The passage has a lot of details so read carefully and stay clear.

36. B
The choices are designed to confuse. Check the text for the exact definition and do not be distracted by other choices.

37. A
Here is a quick tip. On choice A, the word Hypovolemic is used. This is an unusual word and specific medical vocabulary. None of the other choices uses any specific vocabulary like this, so it is very likely to be the right answer. You can quickly scan the text for this word to confirm. Scanning the text for an unusual word is easy and fast, and one of the most powerful techniques for this type of question.

38. C
Scan the text for Zaire.

Strategy 11 - Look at the big picture

Details can be tricky when dealing with main idea and summary questions, but do not let the details distract you. Look at the big picture instead of the smaller parts to determine the right answer.

39. D
The passage says in 2005 it was found there are 3 fruit bat species most suspected of carrying the virus. The details (3 species, fruit bats and 2005) do not matter. Only the fact that bats are suspected.

40. B
The relevant passage is, "Of 24 plant species and 19 vertebrate species experimentally inoculated with Ebola virus, only bats became infected." The inference is that these plant and animal species cannot be infected, (i.e. carry and transmit the disease) so Choice B is correct.

41. A
The relevant passage is, "Bats are also known to be the reservoirs for a number of related viruses including Nipah virus, Hendra virus and Lyssaviruses."

Strategy 12 - Make the best choice based on the information given.

42. B

Choices B and C are incorrect by the passage, "In the early stages, Ebola may not be highly contagious." Choice A is not mentioned, leaving choice D.

43. B

The passage does not say anything about the information in choices A and D. Choice C is irrelevant to the question.

44. A

Choices B and C are not mentioned in the passage. Choice D is a good possibility, however, choice A covers choice D and is referred to in the passage.

45. B

Choice A is incorrect. Choices C and D are not mentioned.

How to Improve your Vocabulary

Vocabulary tests can be daunting when you think of the enormous number of words that might come up in the exam. As the exam date draws near, your anxiety will grow because you know that no matter how many words you memorize, chances are, you will still remember so few, and there are so many more to memorize! Here are some tips which you can use to hurdle the big words that may come up in your exam without having to open the dictionary and memorize all the words known to humankind.

Build up and tear apart the big words. Big words, like many other things, are composed of small parts. Some words are made up of many other words. A man who lifts weights for example, is a weight lifter. Words are also made up of word parts called prefixes, suffixes and roots. Often times, we can see the relationship of different words through these parts. A person who is skilled with both hands is ambidextrous. A word with double meaning is ambiguous. A person with two conflicting emotions is ambivalent. Two words with synonymous meanings often have the same root. Bio, a root word derived from Latin is used in words like biography meaning to write about a person's life, and biology meaning the study of living organisms.

- **Words with double meanings.** Did you know that the word husband not only means a man married to a woman, but also thrift or frugality? Sometimes, words have double meanings. The dictionary meaning, or the denotation of a word is sometimes different from the way we use it or its connotation.

- **Read widely, read deeply and read daily.** The best

way to expand your vocabulary is to familiarize yourself with as many words as possible through reading. By reading, you are able to remember words in a proper context and thus, remember its meaning or at the very least, its use. Reading widely would help you get acquainted with words you may never use every day. This is the best strategy without doubt. However, if you are studying for an exam next week, or even tomorrow, it isn't much help! Below you will find a range of different ways to learn new words quickly and efficiently.

• **Remember.** Always remember that big words are easy to understand when divided into smaller parts, and the smaller words will often have several other meanings aside from the one you already know. Below is an extensive list of root or stem words, followed by one hundred questions to help you learn word stems.

Here are suggested effective ways to help you improve your vocabulary.

Be Committed To Learning New Words. To improve your vocabulary you need to make a commitment to learn new words. Commit to learning at least a word or two a day. You can also get new words by reading books, poems, stories, plays and magazines. Expose yourself to more language to increase the number of new words that you learn.

• **Learn Practical Vocabulary**. As much as possible, learn vocabulary that is associated with what you do and that you can use regularly. For example learn words related to your profession or hobby. Learn as much vocabulary as you can in your favorite subjects.

• **Use New Words Frequently**. As soon as you learn a new word start using it and do so frequently. Repeat it when you are alone and try to use the word as often as you can with people you talk to. You can also use flashcards to practice new words that you learn.

• **Learn the Proper Usage.** If you do not understand the proper usage, look it up and make sure you have it right.

• **Use a Dictionary**. When reading textbooks, novels

or assigned readings, keep the dictionary nearby. Also learn how to use online dictionaries and WORD dictionary. As soon as you come across a new word, check for its meaning. If you cannot do so immediately, then you should right it down and check it as soon as possible. This will help you understand what the word means and exactly how best to use it.

• **Learn Word Roots, Prefixes and Suffixes.** English words are usually derived from suffixes, prefixes and roots, which come from Latin, French or Greek. Learning the root or origin of a word helps you easily understand the meaning of the word and other words that are derived from the root. Generally, if you learn the meaning of one root word, you will understand two or three words. See our List of Stem Words below. This is a great two-for-one strategy. Most prefixes, suffixes, roots and stems are used in two, three or more words, so if you know the root, prefix or suffix, you can guess the meaning of many words.

• **Synonyms and Antonyms**. Most words in the English language have two or three (at least) synonyms and antonyms. For example, "big," in the most common usage, has about seventy-five synonyms and an equal number of antonyms. Understanding the relationships between these words and how they all fit together gives your brain a framework, which makes them easier to learn, remember and recall.

• **Use Flash Cards**. Flash cards are one of the best ways to memorize things. They can be used anywhere and anytime, so you can make use of odd free moments waiting for the bus or waiting in line. Make your own or buy commercially prepared flash cards, and keep them with you all the time.

• **Make word lists.** Learning vocabulary, like learning many things, requires repetition. Keep a new words journal in a separate section or separate notebook. Add any words that you look up in the dictionary, as well as from word lists. Review your word lists regularly.

Photocopying or printing off word lists from the Internet or handouts is not the same. Actually writing out the word and a few notes on the definition is an important process for imprinting the word in your brain. Writing out the word and definition in your New Word Journal, forces you to concentrate and focus on the new word. Hitting PRINT or pushing the button on the photocopier does not do the same thing.

 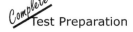

MEANING IN CONTEXT ANSWER SHEET

1. Ⓐ Ⓑ Ⓒ Ⓓ   21. Ⓐ Ⓑ Ⓒ Ⓓ

2. Ⓐ Ⓑ Ⓒ Ⓓ   22. Ⓐ Ⓑ Ⓒ Ⓓ

3. Ⓐ Ⓑ Ⓒ Ⓓ   23. Ⓐ Ⓑ Ⓒ Ⓓ

4. Ⓐ Ⓑ Ⓒ Ⓓ   24. Ⓐ Ⓑ Ⓒ Ⓓ

5. Ⓐ Ⓑ Ⓒ Ⓓ   25. Ⓐ Ⓑ Ⓒ Ⓓ

6. Ⓐ Ⓑ Ⓒ Ⓓ   26. Ⓐ Ⓑ Ⓒ Ⓓ

7. Ⓐ Ⓑ Ⓒ Ⓓ   27. Ⓐ Ⓑ Ⓒ Ⓓ

8. Ⓐ Ⓑ Ⓒ Ⓓ   28. Ⓐ Ⓑ Ⓒ Ⓓ

9. Ⓐ Ⓑ Ⓒ Ⓓ   29. Ⓐ Ⓑ Ⓒ Ⓓ

10. Ⓐ Ⓑ Ⓒ Ⓓ   30. Ⓐ Ⓑ Ⓒ Ⓓ

11. Ⓐ Ⓑ Ⓒ Ⓓ   31. Ⓐ Ⓑ Ⓒ Ⓓ

12. Ⓐ Ⓑ Ⓒ Ⓓ   32. Ⓐ Ⓑ Ⓒ Ⓓ

13. Ⓐ Ⓑ Ⓒ Ⓓ   33. Ⓐ Ⓑ Ⓒ Ⓓ

14. Ⓐ Ⓑ Ⓒ Ⓓ   34. Ⓐ Ⓑ Ⓒ Ⓓ

15. Ⓐ Ⓑ Ⓒ Ⓓ   35. Ⓐ Ⓑ Ⓒ Ⓓ

16. Ⓐ Ⓑ Ⓒ Ⓓ   36. Ⓐ Ⓑ Ⓒ Ⓓ

17. Ⓐ Ⓑ Ⓒ Ⓓ   37. Ⓐ Ⓑ Ⓒ Ⓓ

18. Ⓐ Ⓑ Ⓒ Ⓓ   38. Ⓐ Ⓑ Ⓒ Ⓓ

19. Ⓐ Ⓑ Ⓒ Ⓓ   39. Ⓐ Ⓑ Ⓒ Ⓓ

20. Ⓐ Ⓑ Ⓒ Ⓓ   40. Ⓐ Ⓑ Ⓒ Ⓓ

Meaning in Context

Meaning in context is a powerful tool for learning vocabulary. Essentially, you make an educated guess of the meaning from the context of the sentence. With meaning in context questions, also called sentence completion, you don't have to know the exact meaning - just an approximate meaning to answer the question.

This is also true is when reading. Sometimes it is necessary to know the exact meaning. Other times, the exact meaning is not important and you can make an educated guess from the context and continue reading.

The meaning in context exercises below give you practice making guesses about the meaning.

Directions: For each of the questions below, choose the word with the meaning best suited to the sentence based on the context.

1. When Joe broke his _____ in a skiing accident, his entire leg was in a cast.

    a. Ankle

    b. Humerus

    c. Wrist

    d. Femur

2. Alan had to learn the _____ system of numbering when his family moved to Great Britain.

    a. American

    b. Decimal

    c. Metric

    d. Fingers and toes

3. After Lisa's aunt had her tenth child, Lisa found that she had more than twenty _____.

    a. Uncles

    b. Friends

    c. Stepsisters

    d. Cousins

4. Although he had flown many times, this was his first flight in a _____.

    a. Helicopter

    b. Kite

    c. Train

    d. Subway car

5. George is very serious about his _____, and recently joined the American Scholastic Association.

    a. Schoolwork

    b. Cooking

    c. Travelling

    d. Athletics

6. She was a rabid Red Sox fan, attending every game, and demonstrating her _____ by cheering more loudly than anyone else.

    a. Knowledge

    b. Boredom

    c. Commitment

    d. Enthusiasm

7. When Craig's dog was struck by a car, he rushed his pet to the _____.

    a. Emergency room

    b. Doctor

    c. Veterinarian

    d. Podiatrist

8. After she received her influenza vaccination, Nan thought that she was _____ to the common cold.

    a. Immune

    b. Susceptible

    c. Vulnerable

    d. At risk

9. Paul's rose bushes were being destroyed by Japanese beetles, so he invested in a good _____.

    a. Fungicide

    b. Fertilizer

    c. Sprinkler

    d. Pesticide

10. The last time that the crops failed, the entire nation experienced months of _____.

    a. Famine

    b. Harvest

    c. Plenitude

    d. Disease

11. Because of a pituitary dysfunction, Karl lacked the necessary _____ to grow as tall as his father.

    a. Glands

    b. Hormones

    c. Vitamins

    d. Testosterone

12. Because of its colorful fall _____ , the maple is my favorite tree.

    a. Growth

    b. Branches

    c. Greenery

    d. Foliage

13. When Mr. Davis returned from southern Asia, he told us about the _____ that   sometimes swept the area, bringing torrential rain.

    a. Monsoons

    b. Hurricanes

    c. Blizzards

    d. Floods

14. Is it true that _____ always grows on the north side of trees?

    a. Lichens

    b. Moss

    c. Ferns

    d. Ground cover

15. You can _____ some fires by covering them with dirt, while others require foam or water.

    a. Extinguish

    b. Distinguish

    c. Ignite

    d. Lessen

16. Through the use of powerful fans that circulate the heat over the food, _____ ovens work very efficiently.

    a. Microwave

    b. Broiler

    c. Convection

    d. Pressure

17. Because of the growing use of _____ as a fuel, corn production has greatly increased.

    a. Alcohol

    b. Ethanol

    c. Natural gas

    d. Oil

18. In heavily industrialized areas, the air pollution causes many _____ diseases.

    a. Respiratory

    b. Cardiac

    c. Alimentary

    d. Circulatory

19. Because hydroelectric power is a _____ source of energy, its use is considered a green energy.

 a. Significant

 b. Disposable

 c. Renewable

 d. Reusable

20. The process required the use of highly _____ liquids, so fire extinguishers were everywhere in the factory.

 a. Erratic

 b. Combustible

 c. Inflammable

 d. Neutral

21. I still don't know exactly. That isn't _____ evidence.

 a. Undeterred

 b. Unrelenting

 c. Unfortunate

 d. Conclusive

22. He could manipulate the coins in his fingers very _____.

 a. Brazenly

 b. Eloquently

 c. Boisterously

 d. Deftly

23. His investment scheme _____ many serious investors, who lost money.

    a. Helped

    b. Vindicated

    c. Duped

    d. Reproved

24. When we go to a party, we always _____ a driver.

    a. Feign

    b. Exploit

    c. Dote

    d. Designate

25. This new evidence should _____ any doubts.

    a. Dispel

    b. Dispense

    c. Evaluate

    d. Diverse

26. She went to Asia on $10 a day – her _____ travelling plans are amazing.

    a. Frothy

    b. Frugal

    c. Fraught

    d. Focal

27. My grandmother's house is full or trinkets and ornaments. She is always buying _____.

    a. Collectibles

    b. Baubles

    c. China

    d. Crystal

28. I am finally out of debt! I paid off all of my _____.

    a. Debtors

    b. Defendants

    c. Accounts Receivable

    d. Creditors

29. I love listening to his speeches. He has a gift for _____.

    a. Oratory

    b. Irony

    c. Jargon

    d. None of the above

30. The warehouse went bankrupt so all of the furniture has to be _____.

    a. Dissected

    b. Liquidated

    c. Destroyed

    d. Bought

31. He sold the property when he didn't even own it. The whole thing was a _____.

    a. Hoax

    b. Feign

    c. Defile

    d. Default

32. The repair really isn't working. Those parts you replaced are _____.

    a. Despondent

    b. Illusive

    c. Deficient

    d. Granular

33. Just because she is supervisor, doesn't mean we have to _____ in front of her.

    a. Foible

    b. Grovel

    c. Humiliate

    d. Indispose

34. That noise is _____ ! It is driving me crazy.

    a. Loud

    b. Intolerable

    c. Frivolous

    d. Fictitious

35. Her inheritance was a good size and included many _____.

    a. Heirlooms

    b. Perchance

    c. Cynical

    d. Lateral

36. I see that sign everywhere. It is much more _____ than I thought.

 a. Prelude

 b. Prevalent

 c. Ratify

 d. Rational

37. Her attitude was very casual and _____.

 a. Idle

 b. Nonchalant

 c. Portly

 d. Portend

38. The machine _____ the rock into ore.

 a. Quells

 b. Pulverizes

 c. Eradicates

 d. Segments

39. The water in the pond has been sitting for so long it is _____.

 a. Stagnant

 b. Sediment

 c. Stupor

 d. Residue

40. She didn't listen to a thing and _____ all the objections.

 a. Manipulated

 b. Mired

 c. Furtive

 d. Rebuffed

MEANING IN CONTEXT ANSWER KEY.

1. D
Femur NOUN A thighbone.

2. C
Metric System a system of measurements that is based on the base units of the meter/metre, the kilogram, the second, the ampere, the kelvin, the mole, and the candela.

3. D
Cousins NOUN the son or daughter of a person's uncle or aunt; a first cousin.

4. A
Helicopter

5. B
Schoolwork

6. D
Enthusiasm NOUN intensity of feeling; excited interest or eagerness.

7. C
Veterinarian NOUN medical doctor who treats non-human animals.

8. A
Immune ADJECTIVE protected by inoculation, or due to innate resistance to pathogens.

9. D
Pesticide NOUN a substance, usually synthetic although sometimes biological, used to kill or contain the activities of pests.

10. A
Famine NOUN a period of extreme shortage of food in a region.

11. B
Hormones NOUN any substance produced by one tissue and conveyed by the bloodstream to another to effect physiological activity.

12. D
Foliage NOUN the leaves of plants.

13. A
Monsoons NOUN tropical rainy season when the rain lasts for several months with few interruptions.

14. B
Moss NOUN any of various small green plants growing on the ground or on the surfaces of trees, stones etc.

15. A
Extinguish NOUN to put out, as in fire; to end burning; to quench.

16. C
Convection NOUN the vertical movement of heat and moisture.

17. B
Ethanol NOUN a type of alcohol used as fuel.

18. A
Respiratory NOUN relating to respiration; breathing.

19. D
Reusable NOUN able to be used again; especially after salvaging or special treatment or processing.

20. B
Combustible NOUN capable of burning.

21. D
Conclusive ADJECTIVE providing an end to something; decisive.

22. D
Deftly ADVERB quickly and neatly in action.

23. C
Dupe VERB to swindle, deceive, or trick.

24. D
Designate ADJECTIVE appointed; chosen.

25. A
Dispel VERB to drive away by scattering, or so to cause to vanish; to clear away.

26. B
Frugal ADJECTIVE cheap, economical, thrifty.

27. B
Baubles NOUN a cheap showy ornament.

28. D
Creditors NOUN a person to whom a debt is owed.

29. A
Oratory NOUN the art of public speaking, especially in a formal, expressive, or forceful manner.

30. B
Liquidate VERB to convert assets into cash.

31. A
Hoax NOUN to deceive (someone) by making them believe something which has been maliciously or mischievously fabricated.

32. C
Deficient ADJECTIVE lacking something essential.

33. B
Grovel VERB to abase oneself before another person.

34. B
Intolerable ADJECTIVE not capable of being borne or endured; not proper or right to be allowed; insufferable; insupportable; unbearable.

35. A
Heirloom NOUN A valued possession that has been passed down through the generations.

36. B
Prevalent ADJECTIVE Widespread.

37. B
Nonchalant ADJECTIVE Casually calm and relaxed.

38. B
Pulverizes VERB to completely destroy, especially by crushing to fragments or a powder.

39. A
Stagnant ADJECTIVE lacking freshness, motion, flow, progress, or change; stale; motionless; still.

40. D
Rebuff NOUN a sudden resistance or refusal. [12]

Word List 1 – The Top 100 Common Vocabulary.

Learning vocabulary, especially in a hurry for an exam, means that you will be making friends with a lot of different word lists. Below is a word list of top 100 "must know" vocabulary to get you started.

When studying word lists, think of different ways to mix-it-up. Work with a friend or a study groups and compare word lists and test each other, or make flash cards.

1. **Abate** VERB reduce or lesson.
2. **Abandon** VERB to give up completely.
3. **Aberration** NOUN something unusual, different from the norm.
4. **Abet** VERB to encourage or support.
5. **Abstain** VERB to refrain from doing something.
6. **Abrogate** VERB to abolish or render void.
7. **Aesthetic** ADJECTIVE pertaining to beauty.
8. **Abstemious** ADJECTIVE moderate in the use of food or drink.
9. **Anachronistic** ADJECTIVE out of the context of time, out of date.
10. **Acrimonious** ADJECTIVE sharp or harsh in language or temper.
11. **Asylum** NOUN sanctuary, place of safety.
12. **Banal** ADJECTIVE lacking in freshness, originality, or vigor.
13. **Bias** NOUN a prejudice towards something or against something.
14. **Belie** VERB to give a false idea of.
15. **Brazen** ADJECTIVE bold.
16. **Belligerent** ADJECTIVE engaged in war.
17. **Camaraderie** NOUN togetherness, trust, group dynamic of trust.
18. **Cabal** NOUN a small group of persons engaged in plotting.
19. **Capacious** ADJECTIVE very large, spacious.
20. **Callous** ADJECTIVE unfeeling or insensitive.

Study >> Practice >> Succeed!

21. **Clairvoyant** ADJECTIVE can predict the future.
22. **Cantankerous** ADJECTIVE ill-natured; quarrelsome.
23. **Compassion** NOUN sympathy.
24. **Captious** ADJECTIVE quick to find fault about trifle.
25. **Condescending** ADJECTIVE patronizing.
26. **Chauvinist** NOUN an extreme patriot.
27. **Conformist** NOUN someone who follows the majority.
28. **Clamorous** VERB loud and noisy.
29. **Deleterious** ADJECTIVE harmful.
30. **Deference** NOUN submitting to the wishes or judgment of another.
31. **Digression** NOUN straying from main point.
32. **Delectable** ADJECTIVE very pleasing.
33. **Discredit** NOUN dishonor someone, prove something untrue.
34. **Demeanor** NOUN behavior; bearing.
35. **Divergent** ADJECTIVE moving apart, going in different directions.
36. **Edict** NOUN a public command or proclamation issued by an authority.
37. **Emulate** NOUN following someone else's example.
38. **Effete** ADJECTIVE no longer productive; hence, lacking in or, worn out.
39. **Ephemeral** ADJECTIVE fleeting, temporary.
40. **Elicit** VERB to draw out.
41. **Exemplary** ADJECTIVE outstanding.
42. **Elucidate** VERB to make clear; to explain florid: ornate.
43. **Forbearance** NOUN patience, restraint.
44. **Facade** NOUN front or face, especially of a building.
45. **Fortuitous** ADJECTIVE lucky.
46. **Fallacious** ADJECTIVE unsound; misleading; deceptive.
47. **Fraught** NOUN filled with.
48. **Flaccid** ADJECTIVE lacking firmness.
49. **Ghastly** ADJECTIVE horrible, deathlike.
50. **Grimace** NOUN a distortion of the face to express an attitude or feeling.
51. **Hedonist** NOUN person who acts in pursuit of pleasure.
52. **Harbinger** NOUN a forerunner; ail announcer.
53. **Impetuous** ADJECTIVE rash, impulsive.

54. **Immaculate** ADJECTIVE spotless; pure.
55. **Inconsequential** ADJECTIVE without consequence, trivial, does not matter.
56. **Impeccable** ADJECTIVE faultless.
57. **Intrepid** ADJECTIVE fearless.
58. **Imprecation** NOUN a curse.
59. **Jubilation** NOUN extreme happiness, joy.
60. **Latent** ADJECTIVE hidden; present but not fully developed.
61. **Longevity** NOUN long (particularly long life).
62. **Maudlin** ADJECTIVE sentimental to the point of tears.
63. **Nonchalant** ADJECTIVE casual, calm, at ease.
64. **Oblivious** ADJECTIVE forgetful; absent-minded.
65. **Orator** NOUN speaker.
66. **Obviate** VERB to prevent, dispose of, or make un necessary by appropriate actions.
67. **Parched** ADJECTIVE lacking water, dried up.
68. **Panacea** NOUN a remedy for all ills.
69. **Pragmatic** ADJECTIVE practical.
70. **Paraphrase** VERB to restate the meaning of a passage in other words.
71. **Pretentious** ADJECTIVE being self important, thinking you are better than others.
72. **Pecuniary** ADJECTIVE pertaining to money.
73. **Prosaic** ADJECTIVE ordinary.
74. **Pensive** ADJECTIVE sadly thoughtful.
75. **Provocative** ADJECTIVE causes a fuss, inflammatory, likely to get people riled up.
76. **Peruse** VERB to read carefully.
77. **Querulous** ADJECTIVE irritable, prone to argument.
78. **Radical** NOUN one who advocates extreme basic changes.
79. **Reclusive** ADJECTIVE hermit, withdrawn.
80. **Recapitulate** VERB to restate in a brief, concise form.
81. **Renovate** VERB to make new, being redone.
82. **Refute** VERB to prove incorrect or false.
83. **Reverence** NOUN deep respect.
84. **Sallow** ADJECTIVE sick.
85. **Scrutinize** VERB to look at carefully.
86. **Sanguinary** ADJECTIVE bloody.
87. **Spurious** ADJECTIVE false, untrue.

88. **Scourge** VERB to punish severely; to afflict; to whip.
89. **Substantiate** VERB to confirm, prove.
90. **Scrutinize** VERB to examine carefully.
91. **Superficial** ADJECTIVE shallow.
92. **Sleazy** ADJECTIVE flimsy and cheap.
93. **Surreptitious** ADJECTIVE secret.
94. **Tactful** ADJECTIVE polite.
95. **Tangible** ADJECTIVE real; actual.
96. **Transient** ADJECTIVE temporary, impermanent.
97. **Vanquish** VERB to subdue or conquer.
98. **Vindicate** VERB to free from blame.
99. **Wary** ADJECTIVE careful, watchful.
100. **Zenith** NOUN the highest point.

Word List 2 – Stem Words.

Probably the best way of learning new vocabulary is our "two-for-one" strategy of learning a stem word and then you can recognize two, three or more words that use the stem word. If you are studying for an exam with a vocabulary section, this is the best strategy for you.

Below is an extensive list of stem words with their meaning and examples. Following this list are 100 questions. These are divided into two question styles. In Part I, you are given the stem and asked to choose the meaning, and in Part II you are given the meaning and asked to choose the stem.

A

Root	Meaning	Examples
ab-, a-, abs-	away	abnormal, abrasion, absent, abstract, aversion
ac-, acu-	sharp, pointed	acupuncture
acr(i)-	sharp, pungent	acrid, acrimony
acr(o)-	height, summit	acrobatics, acromegaly, acronym, acrophobia,
ad-, a-, ac-, af-, ag-,al-, ap-, ar-, as-, at-	movement to or toward; in addition	adapt, affect, ascend, accept
aer-, aero-	air, atmosphere	aeronautics, aerosol
aesthet-	feeling, sensation	aesthetics, anaesthetic
agri-, egri	field, country	agriculture, peregrine
am-, amat-, amor-	love, loved,	amateur, amorous

A con't

Root	Meaning	Examples
ambi-	on both sides	ambidexterity, ambivalent
amic-, -imic-	friend	amicable, inimical
ant-, anti-	against, opposed to, preventive	antibiotic, antipodes
ante-, anti-	before, in front of, prior to	antebellum, antediluvian, anticipate, antiquarian
anthropo-	human	anthropology, anthropomor-phic
aqu-	water	aquamarine, aquarium, aque-duct
arche-, archi-	ruler	archangel, archetype
archaeo-, archeo-	ancient	archaeology or archeology, ar-chaic
arthr(o)-	joint	arthritis, arthropod
astr-, astro-	star, star-shaped	asterisk, astrology, astronomy, disaster
athl-	prize	athlete, pentathlon
aud(i)-	hearing, listening, sound	auditorium, auditory
aut- , auto-	self; directed from within	automobile, autonomy
avi-	bird	aviary, aviation

B

Root	Meaning	Examples
bac-	rod-shaped	bacilla, bacteria
baro-	weight, pressure	barometer, barograph,
basi-	at the bottom	basic, basis
bell(i)-	war	bellicose, belligerent
ben-	good, well	benefit, benignity
bi-	two	binoculars, bigamy, biscotti
bibl-	book	bibliography, bible
bi(o)-	life	biology, biologist, biosphere

B con't

Root	Meaning	Examples
brev(i)-	brief, short (time)	abbreviation, brevity
burs-bursa	pouch, purse	bursar, bursary, disburse,

C

Root	Meaning	Examples
calc-	stone	calculus, calcite, calcium
can(i)-	dog	canine, Canis Major
cand-	glowing, iridescent	candid, incandescent, candle, candela
cap-, -cip-, capt-, -cept-	hold, take	capture, captive, conception, recipient
capit-, -cipit-	head	capital, decapitation, precipitation
capr-	goat	Capricorn, caprine
cardi(o)-	relating to the heart	cardiology, cardiograph
carp-	relating to the wrist	carpal, carpal tunnel syndrome
cata-	down	catastrophe, catabolic, cathode,
cav-	hollow	cave, cavity, excavation
ced-, cess-	go	procession, recede
celer-	quick	acceleration, celerity
cent-	hundred	cent, centennial, centurion
cervic-	relating to the neck, relating to the cervix	cervix, cervical
chloro-	green	chlorine, chlorophyll, chloroplast
choreo	dance	choreograph, choreography
chron-	time	chronic, chronometer, chronology
circum-	around	circumference, circumcise
clar-	clear	clarity, declaration
claud-, -clud-, claus-,-clus-	close	clause, exclusion,

C con't

Root	Meaning	Examples
		include
clav-	key	conclave, clavicle
clement-	mild	clemency, inclement
clin-	bed, lean,	recline declination, inclined
cogn-	know	cognitive, cognizant, recognize
con-, co-, col-, com-, cor-	with, together	connect, collide, compress
con(o)-	cone	conic, conical
contra-	against	contrast, contradict ("say against")
cord-	heart	accord, cordial
corn-	horn	cornea, cornucopia, unicorn, cornified
coron-	crown	corona, coronation
corpor-	body	corporation, corpse, corpuscle
cosmet(o)-		cosmetics, cosmetology
cre-	make	creation, creature
cred-	believe, trust	credibility, credentials
cris-, crit-	judge	crisis, critic
cruc(i)-	cross	crucial, crucifix, crucify, excruciating
crypt-	hidden	cryptic, cryptography
cub-	cube	cubic, cuboid
culp-	blame, fault	culpable, exculpate
cune-	wedge	cuneiform

C con't

Root	Meaning	Examples
curr-, curs-	run	concurrent, recursion, cursive, current
cycl(o)-	circular	bicycle, cycle, cyclone

D

Root	Meaning	Examples
damn-, -demn-	to inflict loss	condemn, damnation
de-	from, away from, removing	delete, demented
deca-, dec-, deka-, dek-	Ten	decagram, decahedron
decim-	tenth part	decimal, decimate
dem-, demo-	people	demagogue, democracy
dens-	thick	condense, density
dent-	tooth	dental, dentures
derm-	skin	dermis, epidermis, hypodermic
dia-	apart, through	dialysis, diameter
dict-	say, speak	contradict, dictation, dictionary, edict, predict
doc-, doct-	teach	docile, doctor
dogmat-, dox-	opinion, tenet	dogmatic, orthodox
dorm-	sleep	dormant, dormitory
duc-, duct-	lead	abduction, introduction, production, reduction, deduction
dur-	hard	durable, duration, duress, en-dure

E

Root	Meaning	Examples
eco-	house	ecology, economics,
ego-	self, I (first person)	egocentric
em-, empt-	buy	exemption, redeem
emul-	equal, rivaling	emulator
epi-, ep-	upon	epicenter, epoch
equ-, -iqu-	even, level	equal, equivalence
equ-	horse	Equestrian
erg-	work	ergonomics
err-	stray	aberration, errant
ethn	native	ethnicity, ethnic

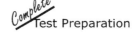

E con't

Root	Meaning	Examples
eu-	well, good	euphoria, euthanasia
ex-, e-, ef-	from, out	exclude, extrude, extend
exo-	outside	exothermic
exter-, extra-	outer	exterior, extrasensory
extrem-	utmost, outermost	extremity, extremophile

F

Root	Meaning	Examples
f-, fat-	say, speak	fate, infant, preface
fac-, -fic-, fact, -fect-	make	defect, factory, manufacture
femin-	female	femininity, feminist
fall-, -fell-, fals	deceive	falsity, infallibility
fatu-	foolish, useless	fatuous, infatuation
feder-	treaty, agreement, contract, league	confederation, federal
fel-	cat	feline
felic-	happy, merry	felicity
fend-, fens-	prevent	defend, offense
fer-	carry	reference, transfer
fid-, fis-	faith, trust	confidence, fidelity
fin-	end	finish, final
find-, fiss-	split	fission, fissures
firm-	fix, settle	confirmation, firmament
fl-	blow	flatulence, inflation
flect-, flex-	bend	flexor, inflection
flig-, flict-	strike	conflict, inflict
flor-	flower	floral, florid
flu-, flux-	flow	effluent, fluency
form-	shape	conformity, deformity, formation
frang-, -fring-, fract-, frag-	break	fracture, fragment, frangible, infringe
frater-, fratr-	brother	fraternity
fric-, frict-	rub	dentifrice, friction

F con't

Root	Meaning	Examples
front-	forehead	confront, frontal
fug-, fugit-	flee refuge	centrifuge, fugitive,
fum-	smoke	fume, fumigation
fund-	bottom	fundamentalism, profundity
fund-, fus-	pour	effusion, profusion
fung-, funct-	do	function, fungibility

G

Root	Meaning	Examples
gastr-	stomach	gastric, gastroenterologist
germin-	sprout	germination
ger-, gest-	bear, carry	digest, gestation
glac-	slow, ice	glacier, glacial
glob-	sphere	global, globule
grad-, -gred-, gress-	walk, step,	grade, regress
gran-	grain	granary, granule
graph-	draw, write	graphic, graphology
greg-	flock	gregarious, segregation
gubern-	govern, pilot	gubernatorial
gymn-	nude	gymnasium, gymnosperm

H

Root	Meaning	Examples
hab-, -hib-, habit-, -hibit-	have	habit, prohibition
haem-	blood	haemophilia, hemoglobin
heli(o)-	sun	heliotrope, helium
hemi-	half	hemicycle, hemisphere
her-, hes-	cling	adhesive, coherent
herb-	grass	herbicide
hod-	way	cathode, hodometer,
hom(o)-	same	homosexual, homogenous
hor-	boundary	aphorism, horizon
hort(i)-	garden	horticulture, horticulturist
hospit-	host	hospitality, hospitable
hum-	ground	exhumation, inhume
hydr(o)-	water	hydrology, hydrophobia,

H con`t

Root	Meaning	Examples
hydr(o)-		hydroponic, hydraulic, hydrlysis, hydrous, hydrophilic
hygr-	wet	hygrometer

I

Root	Meaning	Examples
idi(o)-	personal	idiom, idiosyncrasy, idiot
ign-	fire	igneous, ignition
in- (1), im-	in, on	incur, intend, invite
in- (2), il-, im-, ir-	not	
	un- (negation)	illicit, impossible, irrational
infra-	below, under	infrastructure, infrared
insul-	island	insular, insulation
inter-	among, between	intercollegiate, intermission, intersection
irasc-, irat-	be angry	irascible, irate
is-, iso-	equal, the same	isometric, isomorphic, isotropic

J

Root	Meaning	Examples
jac- -ject-	cast, throw	eject, interject, ejaculate, trajectory
joc-	joke	jocularity
jug-	yoke	conjugal, subjugate
jung-, junct-	join	conjunction, juncture
janu-	door	janitor
jus-, jur-, judic-	law, justice	justice, jury, judge
juven-	young, youth	juvenile, rejuvenate
juxta-	beside, near	juxtaposition

K

Root	Meaning	Examples
kil(o)-	thousand	kilobyte, kilogram, kilometer
kine-	movement, motion	telekinesis, kinetic kinesthetic
klept-	steal	kleptomania
kudo-	glory	kudos

L

Root	Meaning	Examples
lab-, laps-	slide, slip	elapse, relapse
labi-	lip	bilabial, labial
labor-	toil	collaboration, elaboration
lacer-	tear	laceration, lacerate
lact-	milk	lactate, lactation, lactose
lamin-	layer, slice	laminate, lamination
larg-	large	enlargement, largess
larv-	ghost, mask	larva, larvae, larval
lax-	not tense	laxative, relaxation
leg-	law	legal, legislative
leon-	lion	Leo, leonine, Leopold
-less	lack of	penniless
lev-	lift, light	elevator, levitation
liber-	free	liberation, liberty
lig-	bind	ligament, ligature
lin-	line	linearity, line
lingu-	language, tongue	bilingual, linguistic
liter-	letter	alliteration, illiterate,
lith(o)-	stone	lithosphere, megalith, monolith, Neolithic Era
loc-	place	local, location
long-	long	elongate, longitude
loqu-, locut-	speak	allocution, eloquence
luc-	bright, light	Lucifer (bearer of light)
lud-, lus-	play	allude, illusion
lumin-	light	illumination, luminous
lun-	moon	lunar, lunatic
lysis	dissolving	analysis, cytolysis, hydrolysis

M

Root	Meaning	Examples
magn-	great, large	magnanimous, magnificent
maj-	greater	majesty, majority, majuscule
mal-	bad, wretched	malfeasance, malicious, malignancy
mamm-	breast	mammal, mammary gland
man-	stay	immanence

Study >> Practice >> Succeed!

M con`t

Root	Meaning	Examples
mand-	hand	mandate, remand
mania	mental illness	kleptomania, maniac
manu-	hand	manual, manuscript
mar-	sea	marine, maritime
mater-, matr-	mother	matriarch, matrix
maxim-	greatest	maximal, maximum
medi-, -midi-	middle	median, medieval
men(o)-	moon	menopause, menstruation
ment-	mind	demented, mentality
merc-	reward, wages	mercantile, merchant
merg-, mers-	dip, plunge	emerge, immersion
mes-	middle	mesolithic, mesozoic
meter-, metr-	measure	metric, thermometer
meta-	above, among, beyond	metaphor, metaphysical
micr(o)-	small	microphone, microscope
migr-	wander	emigrant, migrate
milit-	soldier	military, militia
mill-	thousand	millennium, million
mim-	repeat	mime, mimic
min-	less, smaller	minority, minuscule
mir-	wonder, amazement	admire, miracle, mirror
mis-	hate	misandry, misogyny
misce-, mixt-	mix	miscellaneous, mixture
mitt-, miss-	send	intermittent, missionary, transmission
mne-	memory	mnemonic
moll-	soft	emollient, mollify
mon(o)-	one	monolith, monotone
mont-	mountain	Montana
morph-	form, shape	anthropomorphism, morpheme, morphology
mort-	death	immortal, mortality, mortuary
mov-, mot-	move	motion mobile, momentum, motor, move
mulg-, muls-	milk	emulsion
mult(i)-	many, much	multiple, multiplex, multitude
mur-	wall	immured, mural
myth(o)-	story	mythic, mythology

Study >> Practice >> Succeed!    *Complete* Test Preparation

N

Root	Meaning	Examples
narc-	numb	narcosis, narcotic
nas-	nose	nasal
nav-	ship	naval, navigate
neur-	nerve	neurology, neurosurgeon
nod-	knot	node, nodule
nov-	new	innovation, nova
nud-	naked	denude, nudity
nutri	nourish	nutrition, nutrient

O

Root	Meaning	Examples
ob-, o-, oc-, os-	against	obstinate, ostentatious, obstreperous
oct-	eight	octagon, octahedron
oct-	eight	octangular, octennial, octovir
octav-	eighth	octaval, octave
ocul-	eye	ocular, oculus
odor	smell	odorous, malodorous
omni-	all	omnipotence, omnivore
ophthalm-	eye	ophthalmology
opt-	eye	optical, optician
opt-	choose	adopt, optional
optim-	best	optimum
or-	mouth	oral, orator
ordin-	order	ordinal, ordinary
orn-	decorate	adorn, ornament, ornate
orth(o)-	straight	orthodoxy, orthosis
osteo-	bone	osteoporosis
ov-	egg	oval, ovule

P

Root	Meaning	Examples
pac-	peace	pacifism, pacifist
paed-, ped	child	paediatric, paedictrician
pagin-	page	pagination, paginate
pal-	stake	impalement, pale
pall-	be pale	pallid, pallor
pand-, pans-	spread	expand, expansion
par(a)-	beside, near	parallel, parameter
part(i)-	part	bipartite, partition

P con't

Root	Meaning	Examples
parthen(o)-	maiden	parthenogenesis
pasc-, past-	feed	pasture, repast
path-	feel, hurt	pathetic, pathology
pati-, pass-	suffer, feel, endure, permit	passive, patience
ped-	foot, child	pedal, quadruped, pediatric
pell-, puls-	drive	propellent, propulsor, repellent
pen-	almost	peninsula, penultimate, penumbra
pent-	five	pentagon
pept-	to digest	peptic, peptide
per-	thoroughly, through	perfection, persistence
peri-	around	perimeter, periscope
pet-	strive towards	appetite, competition
pharmac-	drug, medicine	pharmacy, pharmacist
phob-	fear	hydrophobia agoraphobia
phon(o)-	sound	homophone, microphone, phonograph
phos-, phot-	light	phosphor, photograph
plac-, -plic-	please	placebo, placid
plan-	flat	explanation, planar, plane
plas-	mould	plasma, plastic
plaud-, -plod-, plaus-, -plos-	clap	applaud, applause, explosion, implode
ple-, plet-	fill	complement, suppletion
plic-	fold	duplication, replicate
plum-	feather	plumage, plumate
pod-	foot	podiatry, tripod
pol-	pole	dipole, polar
pole-, poli-	city	metropolis, politics
pon-, posit-	put	component, position, postpone
ponder-	weight	preponderance
port-	carry	export, transportation
post-	after, behind	posterior, postscript
potam-	river	Mesopotamia, hippopotamus

Study >> Practice >> Succeed!

P con't

Root	Meaning	Examples
pre-	before	prehistoric, previous
prim-	first	primary, primeval, primitive
prior-	former	priority
priv(i)-	separate	deprivation, privilege
proxim-	nearest	approximate, proximity
pubi-	sexually mature	pubescent, pubic
pugn-	fight	pugnacious, repugnant
pung-, punct-	prick	puncture, pungent
pup-	doll	pupa, puppet

Q

Root	Meaning	Examples
quadr-	four	quadrangle, quadrillion
quart-	fourth	quartary, quartile
quatern-	four each	quaternary, quaternion
quer-, -quir-, quesit-, -quisit-	search, seek	inquisition, query
quint-	fifth	quintary, quintile
quot-	how many, how great	quota, quotient

R

Root	Meaning	Examples
rad-, ras-	scrape, shave	abrade, abrasion
radi-	beam, spoke	radiance, radiation
ram-	branch	ramification, ramose
ranc-	rancidness, grudge, bitterness	rancid, rancor
rauc-	harsh, hoarse	raucous
re-, red-	again, back	recede, redact
reg-, -rig-, rect-	straight	dirigible, erect, erection, rectum
ren-	kidney	renal
rep-, rept-	crawl, creep	reptile

Study >> Practice >> Succeed!

Complete Test Preparation

R con't

Root	Meaning	Examples
retro-	backward, behind	retrograde, retrospective, retrovirus
rid-, ris-	laugh	derision, ridicule
rod-, ros-	gnaw	corrode, erosion, rodent
ruber-, rubr-	red	rubric, ruby
rump-, rupt-	break	eruption, rupture

S

Root	Meaning	Examples
sacchar-	sugar	saccharin
sacr-, secr-	sacred	consecrate, sacrament
sagitt-	arrow	sagittal plane, Sagittaria
sal-	salt	salinity
sali-, -sili-, salt-	jump	resilient, salient,
san-	healthy	insane, sanity
sanc-	holy	sanctify, sanctuary
sanguin-	blood	consanguinity, sanguine
sapi-, -sipi-	taste, wise	incipience, sapient
saur-	lizard, reptile	dinosaur
scab-	scratch	scabies
scal-	ladder, stairs	scalar, scale
scand-, -scend-, scans-, -scens-	climb	ascend, transcendent
sci-	know	prescient, science
scind-, sciss-	split	rescind, scissors
scop-, scept-	look at, examine, view, observe	horoscope, kaleidoscope, stethoscope
scrib-, script-	write	inscribe, scripture
se-, sed-	apart	secede, sedition
sec-, sect-, seg-	cut	section, segment
sed-	settle, calm	sedative, sedate
sed-, -sid-, sess-	sit	reside, sediment, session, supersede
sema-	sign	semantics, semaphore
sen-	old man	senator, senility
senti-, sens-	feel	consensus, sentient

S con't

Root	Meaning	Examples
sequ-, secut-	follow	consecutive, sequence
serp-	crawl, creep	serpent
serv-	save, protect	conservation
set-	bristle, hair	seta, setose
sever-	stern, strict, serious	severity
sign-	sign	design, designate, signal
sil-	quiet or still	silence
silv(i)-	forest	silviculture
simi-	ape, monkey	simian
simil-	likeness, trust, group	assimilate, similarity
simul-	imitating, feigning	simulation
singul-	one each	singular
sinu-	(to draw) a line	insinuate
siph(o)-	tube	siphon
sist-	cause to stand	consist, persistence
soci-	group	associate, social
sol-	sun	solar
sol-	comfort	soothe, consolation
sol-	alone, only	desolate, sole, solo, solipsism
solv-, solut-	loosen, set free	dissolve, solution
soma-	body	somatic
somn-	sleep	insomnia
son-	sound	resonance
soph-	wise	sophist
sorb-, sorpt-	suck	absorb, absorption
sord-	dirt	sordid
soror-	sister	sorority
spati-	space	spatial
spec-, -spic-, spect-	look	conspicuous, inspection, specimen
spect-	watch, look at	spectator
specul-	observe	speculation

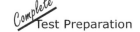

S con't

Root	Meaning	Examples
sper-	hope	desperation, esperance
spher-	ball	sphere, spheroid
spir-	breathe	respiration
squal-	scaly, dirty, filthy	squalid, squalor
st-	stand	stable, station, status, statistic, statue
stagn-	pool of standing water	stagnant
statu-, -stitu-	stand	institution, statute
stell-	star	constellation, stellar
still-	drip	distillation
stimul-	goad, rouse, excite	stimulate
stingu-, stinct-	apart	distinction, distinguish
string-, strict-	upright, stiff	stringent
stru-, struct-	structure , building	construction, construe
stud-	dedication	student
stup-	wonder	stupor
styl-	column, pillar	stylus
su-, sut-	sew	suture
sui-	self	suicide
suad-, suas-	urge	persuasion
suav-	sweet	suave
sub-, su-, sus-	below	submerge
subter-	under	subterfuge, subterranean
sum-, sumpt-	take	assumption, consume
supra-	above, over	supranationalism
syn-, sy-, syl-, sym-	with	symbol, symmetry, synonym, system

T

Root	Meaning	Examples
tac-, -tic-	be silent	reticent, tacit

Complete Test Preparation

T con`t

Root	Meaning	Examples
tach-	swift	tachometer
tang-, -ting-, tact-, tag-	touch	contact, tactile, tangent
tard-	slow	retard
techn-	art, skill	technology
teg-, tect-	cover	integument, protection
tele-	far, end	telegram, telephone, telescope
tempor-	time	contemporary, temporal, temporary
ten-, -tin-, tent-	hold	continent, detention, tenacious, tenor
tend-, tens-	stretch	extend, extension
tenu-	slender, thin	attenuate, tenuous
ter-, trit-	rub	attrition, contrite
termin-	boundary, limit, end	determine, terminal, termination
terr-	dry land	terrace, terracotta, terrain
terti-	third	tertian, tertiary
test-	witness	testament, testimony
tetr-	four	tetrahedron
tex-, text-	weave	texture, textile
than-	death	euthanasia
the-	put	theme, thesis
the(o)-, thus-	god	theology, enthusiasm
therm-	heat, warm	thermometer, endotherm
tim-	be afraid	timid
ting-, tinct-	moisten	tincture
ton-	stretch	tone, isotonic
top-	place	topic, topography
torqu-, tort-	twist	extortion, torque, torture
tot-	all, whole	total, totality
trans-, tra-, tran-	across	tradition, transcend, transportation
trapez-	four-sided, table	trapezoid trapezius
traum-	wound	trauma, traumatic
tri-	three	triad, tripod

T con`t

Root	Meaning	Examples
tri-	three	triangle, trivia, triumvirate
trud-, trus-	thrust	extrusion, intrude
typ-	stamp, model	archetype, phenotype, typography

U

Root	Meaning	Examples
ultim-	farthest	ultimatum, ultimate
umbilic	navel	umbilical
umbr-	shade, shadow	penumbra, umbrella
un-, uni-	one	unary, union
und-	wave	abundant, undulate
urb-	city	urban
ut-, us-	use	usual, utility

V

Root	Meaning	Examples
vac-	empty	vacancy, vacation, vacuum
vad-, vas-	go	evade, pervasive
vag-	wander	vague, vagabond
vap-	lack (of)	evaporation, vapid, vaporize
veh-, vect-	carry	vehicle, vector
vel-	veil	revelation, velate
ven-, vent-	come	advent, convention
vend-	sell	vendor, vending
vener-	respectful	veneration, venereal
vent-	wind	ventilation
ver-	true	verify, verity
verb-	word	verbal, verbatim, verbosity
verber-	whip	reverberation
vert-, vers-	turn	convert, inversion, invert, vertical
vest-	clothe, garment	divest, vest
vestig-	follow, track	investigate
veter-	old	inveterate, veteran
vi-	way	deviate, obvious, via
vic-	change	vice versa, vicissitude
vid-, vis-	see	video, vision
vil-	cheap	vile, vilify

V con't

Root	Meaning	Examples
vinc-, vict-	conquer	invincible, victory
viti-	fault	vice, vitiate
viv-	live	revive, survive, vivid
voc-	voice	vocal, vocation, provocative
volv-, volut-	roll	convolution, revolve
vor-, vorac-	swallow	devour, voracious
vulg-	common, crowd	divulge, vulgarity, vulgate

X

Root	Meaning	Examples
xen-	foreign	xenophobia

Z

Root	Meaning	Examples
zo-	animal, living being	protozoa, zoo, zoology
zon-	belt, girdle	zone
zym-	ferment	enzyme, lysozyme [11]

Stem Words Practice Questions
Part I.

1. Choose the meaning of the stem word agri-

   a. Markings

   a. Development

   a. Field

   a. Government

2. Choose the meaning of the stem word ambi-

   a. Health study

   b. Cellular tissue

   c. Stretched out

   d. On both sides

3. Choose the meaning of the stem word baro-

   a. Weight or pressure

   b. North

   c. Brief

   d. Greatness

4. Choose the meaning of the stem word bibl-

   a. At the bottom

   b. Deep

   c. Book

   d. Wood

5. Choose the meaning of the stem word calc-

    a. Pretty

    b. Stone

    c. Weak

    d. Vault

6. Choose the meaning of the stem word cand-

    a. Long

    b. Goat like

    c. Harden

    d. Glowing

7. Choose the meaning of the stem word damn-

    a. To inflict loss upon

    b. Tenth part

    c. Leadership

    d. Move away from

8. Choose the meaning of the stem word derm-

    a. Above

    b. Skin

    c. Insane actions

    d. Fingers

9. Choose the meaning of the stem word emul-

    a. View

    b. In support

    c. Striving to equal

    d. Against

10. Choose the meaning of the stem word fatu-

    a. Shape

    b. Foolish or useless

    c. Wind direction

    d. Size

11. Choose the meaning of the stem word equ-

    a. Even or level

    b. Knowledge

    c. Inside or within

    d. House

12. Choose the meaning of the stem word fel-

    a. Opportunity

    b. Widow

    c. Female

    d. Cat

13. Choose the meaning of the stem word gastr-

    a. Stomach

    b. Formality

    c. Appearance

    d. Related to health

14. Choose the meaning of the stem word germin-

    a. Small animals

    b. Race

    c. Sprout

    d. Ice

15. Choose the meaning of the stem word haem-

    a. Mental state

    b. Blood

    c. Child health

    d. Time

16. Choose the meaning of the stem word hemi-

    a. Half

    b. Air

    c. Strange

    d. Foreign

17. Choose the meaning of the stem word infra-

    a. Doubtful

    b. Foundation

    c. Strength

    d. Below or under

18. Choose the meaning of the stem word insul-

    a. Angry state

    b. Puncturing

    c. Island

    d. Again

19. Choose the meaning of the stem word janu-

    a. Law

    b. Yoke

    c. Door

    d. Direction

20. Choose the meaning of the stem word junct-

    a. Sound

    b. Join

    c. Jungle

    d. Electricity

21. Choose the meaning of the stem word klept-

    a. General

    b. Shy person

    c. Lawful

    d. Steal

22. Choose the meaning of the stem word -less

    a. Fast in movement

    b. Lack of

    c. Related to dressing or grooming

    d. Advantage over

23. Choose the meaning of the stem word kudo-

    a. Force

    b. Thousand

    c. Glory

    d. Inflammation

24. Choose the meaning of the stem word labi-

    a. Lips

    b. Layers

    c. Delay

    d. Secure

25. Choose the meaning of the stem word lact-

    a. Shine

    b. Milk

    c. Lecture

    d. Teaching

26. Choose the meaning of the stem word lingu-

    a. Teacher

    b. Language, tongue

    c. Knowledge

    d. Tribes

27. Choose the meaning of the stem word magn-

    a. Hand

    b. Breast

    c. Small in size

    d. Great, large

28. Choose the meaning of the stem word mamm-

    a. Breast

    b. Bad

    c. Stay

    d. Long

29. Choose the meaning of the stem word nas-

    a. Large ship

    b. Death

    c. Foot

    d. Nose

30. Choose the meaning of the stem word nav-

   a. Slime

   b. Ship

   c. Join

   d. Tell

31. Choose the meaning of the stem word octav-

   a. Fearless

   b. Against

   c. Eye

   d. Eighth

32. Choose the meaning of the stem word odor-

   a. Fragrance

   b. Creepy

   c. Sad

   d. Shady

33. Choose the meaning of the stem word optim-

   a. Order

   b. Best

   c. Swing

   d. Straight

34. Choose the meaning of the stem word pac-

   a. Feed

   b. Ancient

   c. Peace

   d. Maiden

35. Choose the meaning of the stem word patr-

    a. Endure

    b. Father

    c. Few

    d. Money

36. Choose the meaning of the stem word pent-

    a. Five

    b. Control

    c. Around

    d. Properly

37. Choose the meaning of the stem word pup-

    a. Four

    b. Doll

    c. Punish

    d. Wolf

38. Choose the meaning of the stem word quart-

    a. Fourth

    b. Quiet

    c. Rest

    d. Milk

39. Choose the meaning of the stem word rauc-

    a. Crawl or creep

    b. Root

    c. Harsh or hoarse

    d. Originate

40. Choose the meaning of the stem word rept-

    a. Mental illness

    b. Creep or crawl

    c. Repetition

    d. Timely

41. Choose the meaning of the stem word retro-

    a. Backward or behind

    b. Air less

    c. Kidney

    d. Nose or snout

42. Choose the meaning of the stem word rupt-

    a. Gnaw

    b. Prow

    c. Throat

    d. Break

43. Choose the meaning of the stem word sal-

    a. Anger

    b. Salt

    c. Jump

    d. Save

44. Choose the meaning of the stem word sacr-

    a. Sacred

    b. Flesh

    c. Scratch

    d. Seriousness

45. Choose the meaning of the stem word saur-

    a. Surround

    a. Fish

    a. Reptile or lizard

    a. Ladder

46. Choose the meaning of the stem word tard-

    a. Slow

    b. Shy

    c. Touch

    d. Hard

47. Choose the meaning of the stem word techn-

    a. Improvement

    b. Shocking

    c. Art, skill

    d. Complete

48. Choose the meaning of the stem word termin-

    a. God

    b. Machine

    c. Boundary or end

    d. Weave

49. Choose the meaning of the stem word therm-

    a. Heat or warm

    b. Beast

    c. Ice

    d. Regulator

50. Choose the meaning of the stem word ultim-

    a. Fruitful

    b. Farthest

    c. Infection

    d. Shadow

STEM VOCABULARY QUESTIONS ANSWER KEY – PART I.

1. C
The stem word agri- means relating to field, for example agriculture.

2. D
The stem word ambi- means on both sides, for example ambivalent.

3. A
The stem word baro- means relating to weight or pressure, for example barometer.

4. C
The stem word bibl- relates to books, for example bibliography and bible.

5. B The stem word calc- means stone, for example calcium.

6. D
The stem word cand- means glowing, for examples candle and candid.

7. A
The stem word damn- means to inflict loss upon, for example condemn and damnation.

8. B
The stem word derm- relates to skin, for example dermis and epidermis.

9. C
The stem word emul- means striving to equal, for example emulation.

10. B
The stem word fatu- means foolish or useless, for example fatuous and infatuation.

11. A

The stem word equ- means even or level, for example equal.

12. D

The stem word fel- means relating to cat, for example feline.

13. A

The stem word gastr- means leading, for example gastric.

14. C

The stem word germin- means sprout, for example germination.

15. B

The stem word haem- means blood, for example hemophilia.

16. A

The stem word hemi- means half, for example hemisphere.

17. D

The stem word infra- means below and under, for example infrastructure.

18. C

The stem word insul- means island, for example insulate.

19. C

The stem word janu- means door, for example janitor.

20. B

The stem word junct- means join, for example junction.

21. D

The stem word klept- means steal, for example kleptomaniac.

22. B

The stem word -less means lack of, for example useless and homeless.

23. C

The stem word kudo- means glory, for example kudos.

24. A

The stem word labi- means lips, for example labial.

25. B

The stem word lact- means milk, for example lactate.

26. B

The stem word lingu- means relating to language, tongue, for example bilingual and linguistic.

27. D

The stem word magn- means great, large, for example magnanimous and magnificent.

28. A

The stem word mamm- means breast, for example mammal.

29. D

The stem word nas- means nose, for example nasal.

30. B

The stem word nav- means ship, for example naval.

31. D

The stem word octav- means eighth, for examples octaval.

32. A

The stem word odor- means fragrance, for example odorous.

33. B

The stem word optim- means best, for example optimum and optimal.

34. C

The stem word pac- means peace, for example pact and pacify.

35. B

The stem word patr- means father, for example patriarch.

36. A

The stem word pent- means five, for example pentagon.

37. B
The stem word pup- means doll, for example puppet.

38. A
The stem word quart- means fourth, for example quartile.

39. C
The stem word rauc- means harsh or hoarse, for example raucous.

40. B
The stem word rept- means to crawl or creep, for example reptile.

41. A
The stem word retro- means backward or behind, for example retrospect and retrograde.

42. D
The stem word rupt- means break, for example rupture.

43. B
The stem word sal- means salt, for example salinity or saline.

44. A
The stem word sacr- means sacred, for example consecrate and sacrament.

45. C
The stem word saur- means reptile or lizard, for example dinosaur.

46. A
The stem word tard- means slow, for example retard or tardy.

47. C
The stem word techn- means art, skill, for example technician.

48. C
The stem word termin- means boundary or end, for exam-

ples termination and terminal.

49. A

The stem word therm- means heat or warm, for example thermal and thermostat.

50. B

The stem word ultim- means farthest, for example ultimate.[11]

Stem Words Practice Part II.

1. Choose the stem word that means air or atmosphere.

   a. Bran-

   b. Gen-

   c. Aero-

   d. Agog-

2. Choose the stem word that means love, loved.

   a. Amor-

   b. Cand-

   c. Glan-

   d. Mania-

3. Choose the stem word that means women, female.

   a. Fam-

   b. Ward-

   c. Gust-

   d. Femin-

4. Choose the stem word that means end.

   a. Gran-

   b. Fin-

   c. Flux-

   d. Eur-

5. Choose the stem word that means life.

   a. Bio-

   b. Calcu-

   c. Ext-

   d. Ago-

Complete Test Preparation

6. Choose the stem word that means outermost, utmost.

    a. Frug-

    b. Etym-

    c. Larg-

    d. Extrem-

7. Choose the stem word that means at the bottom.

    a. Trid-

    b. Eco-

    c. Basi-

    d. Ful-

8. Choose the stem word that means relating to the heart.

    a. Cardio-

    b. Hea-

    c. Dimu-

    d. Gel-

9. Choose the stem word that means relating to dance.

    a. Dan-

    b. Fund-

    c. Choreo-

    d. Andr-

10. Choose the stem word that means finger, toe, digit.

    a. Horti-

    b. Dactyl-

    c. Calcu-

    d. Drim-

11. Choose the stem word that means tenth part.

    a. Decim-

    b. Tenr-

    c. Frug-

    d. Hect-

12. Choose the stem word that means self, I (first person).

    a. Ere-

    b. Ego-

    c. Selfi-

    d. Manu-

13. Choose the stem word that means ice.

    a. Tor-

    b. Janu-

    c. Cool-

    d. Glaci-

14. Choose the stem word that means host.

    a. Hospit-

    b. Habi-

    c. Proc-

    d. Paci-

15. Choose the stem word that means grass.

    a. Frau-

    b. Lea-

    c. Herb-

    d. Le-

16. Choose the stem word that means people, race, tribe, nation.

     a. Adul-

     b. Baro-

     c. Cad-

     d. Ethn-

17. Choose the stem word that means idea; thought.

     a. Cupl(u)-

     b. Stat-

     c. Ide(o)-

     d. Anal-

18. Choose the stem word that means among, between.

     a. Chang-

     b. Sta-

     c. Inter-

     d. Less-

19. Choose the stem word that means young, youth.

     a. Juven-

     b. Yot-

     c. Drap-

     d. Rabi-

20. Choose the stem word that means not tense.

     a. Hommi-

     b. Lax-

     c. –Tic

     d. Tens-

21. Choose the stem word that means mental illness.

    a. Kilm-

    b. Cher-

    c. Mania-

    d. Logy-

22. Choose the stem word that means greater.

    a. Cede-

    b. Culp-

    c. Maj-

    d. Lar-

23. Choose the stem word that means light.

    a. Lumin-

    b. Radi-

    c. Scope-

    d. Promu-

24. Choose the stem word that means nourish.

    a. Phon-

    b. Feast-

    c. Nal-

    d. Nutri-

25. Choose the stem word that means eight.

    a. Kine-

    b. Zeb-

    c. Oct-

    d. Puin-

26. Choose the stem word that means movement, motion.

    a. Kis-

    b. Kine-

    c. Trid-

    d. Agog-

27. Choose the stem word that means child.

    a. Dropi-

    b. Calp-

    c. Ped-

    d. Small-

28. Choose the stem word that means fifth.

    a. Quint-

    b. Ward-

    c. Caldi-

    d. Scor-

29. Choose the stem word that means kidney.

    a. Crop-

    b. Tic-

    c. Mia-

    d. Ren-

30. Choose the stem word that means scratch.

    a. Pus-

    b. Scab-

    c. Hetro-

    d. -Agog

31. Choose the stem word that means three.

    a. Hank-

    b. Qua-

    c. Tri-

    d. Quart-

32. Choose the stem word that means navel.

    a. Umbilic-

    b. Hyal-

    c. Infra-

    d. Ful-

33. Choose the stem word that means city.

    a. Macro-

    b. Larv-

    c. Jac-

    d. Urb-

34. Choose the stem word that means empty.

    a. Odor-

    b. Vac-

    c. Mar-

    d. Nema-

35. Choose the stem word that means respectful.

    a. Ocul-

    b. Nunci-

    c. Vener-

    d. Pecum-

36. Choose the stem word that means foreign.

    a. Xen-

    b. Fora-

    c. Crati-

    d. Lanu-

37. Choose the stem word that means animal, living being.

    a. Ery-

    b. Brat(o)-

    c. Anis-

    d. Zo-

38. Choose the stem word that means save, protect, and serve.

    a. Tor-

    b. Ony-

    c. Serv-

    d. Pall-

39. Choose the stem word that means before.

    a. Hered-

    b. Pre-

    c. Part-

    d. Jug-

40. Choose the stem word that means bone.

    a. Osteo-

    b. Hirsut-

    c. Onym-

    d. Scien-

41. Choose the stem word that means tear.

    a. Lacer-

    b. Hod-

    c. Lapid-

    d. Mand-

42. Choose the stem word that means be angry.

    a. Calcu-

    b. Irat-

    c. Ped-

    d. Gram-

43. Choose the stem word that means end.

    a. Grou-

    b. Stari-

    c. Fin-

    d. Ladi-

44. Choose the stem word that means outside.

    a. Exo-

    b. Deca-

    c. Derac-

    d. Huri-

45. Choose the stem word that means word.

    a. Nauti-

    b. Baro-

    c. Justi-

    d. Verb-

46. Choose the stem word that means sphere.

   a. Curv-

   b. Glob-

   c. Blob-

   d. Derog-

47. Choose the stem word that means prize.

   a. Athl-

   b. Grad-

   c. Baco-

   d. Infi-

48. Choose the stem word that means hollow.

   a. Infor-

   b. Bio-

   c. Cav-

   d. Logy-

49. Choose the stem word that means wet.

   a. Hygr-

   b. Justi-

   c. Quac-

   d. Hedron-

50. Choose the stem word that means joke.

   a. Funi-

   b. Archy-

   c. Ward-

   d. Joc-

STEM WORD ANSWER KEY PART II.

1. C

The stem root word aero- means air, atmosphere, for example, aeronautics and aerosol.

2. A

The stem root word amor- means love, loved, for example amorous.

3. D

The stem root word femin- means relating to women, female, for example femininity.

4. B

The stem root word fin-means end, for example finish and final.

5. A

The stem root word bi(o)- means life, for example, biology, biologist and biosphere.

6. D

The stem root word extrem- means outermost, utmost, for example extremity.

7. C

The stem root word basi- means at the bottom, for example basic and basis.

8. A

The stem root word cardi(o)- means heart, for example cardiology, cardiograph.

9. C

The stem root word choreo- means dance, for example choreography.

10. B

The stem root word dactyl- means finger, toe, digit, word, for example pterodactyl.

11. A

The stem root word decim- means relating to tenth part, for example decimal and decimate.

12. B

The stem root word ego- means relating to self, I (first person), for example egocentric.

13. D

The stem root word glaci- means relating to ice, for example glacier.

14. A

The stem root word hospit- means host, for example hospitality.

15. C

The stem root word herb- means grass, for example, herbicide.

16. D

The stem root word ethn- means people, race, tribe, nation, for example ethnic and ethnicity.

17. C

The stem root word ide(o)- means power, for example ideogram and ideology.

18. C

The stem root word inter- means among or between, for example intercollegiate, intermission and intersection.

19. A

The stem root word juven- means young or youth, for example juvenile, rejuvenate.

20. B

The stem root word lax- means not tense, for example laxative and relaxation.

21. C

The stem root word mania- means relating to mental illness, for example kleptomania and maniac.

 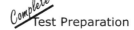

22. C

The stem root word maj- means greater, for example majesty, majority.

23. A

The stem root word lumin- means light, for example illumination and luminous.

24. D

The stem root word nutri- means nourish, for example nutrient.

25. C

The stem root word oct- means eight, for example octagon and octahedron.

26. B

The stem root word kine- means air movement, motion, for example telekinesis, kinetic energy and kinesthetic.

27. C

The stem root word ped- means child, for example pedagogy.

28. A

The stem root word quint- means fifth, for example quinary and quintet.

29. D

The stem root word ren- means kidney, for example renal.

30. B

The stem root word scab- means scratch for example scabies.

31. C

The stem root word tri- means three for example triad and tripod.

32. A

The stem root word umbilic- means navel, for example umbilical.

33. D

The stem root word urb- means city, for example urban.

34. B

The stem root word vac- means empty, for example vacancy, vacation and vacuum.

35. C

The stem root word vener- means respectful, word, for example veneration and venereal.

36. A

The stem root word xen- means foreign, for example xenophobia.

37. D

The stem root word zo- means animal, living being, for example, protozoa, zoo and zoology.

38. C

The stem root word serv- means save, protect, serve, for example conservation.

39. B

The stem root word pre- means before, for example previous.

40. D

The stem root word osteo- means relating to bone, for example osteoporosis.

41. A

The stem root word lacer- means tear, for example laceration.

42. B

The stem root word irat- means anger for example irate.

43. C

The stem root word fin- means relating to end, for example finish and final.

44. A

The stem root word exo- means relating to outside, for ex-

ample exothermic.

45. D

The stem root word verb- means relating to word, for example verbal, verbatim, verbosity.

46. B

The stem root word glob- means relating to sphere, for example global and globule.

47. A

The stem root word athl- means relating to prize, for example athlete, triathlon.

48. C

The stem root word cav- means relating to hollow, for example cave, cavity and excavation.

49. A

The stem root word hygr- means relating to wet, for example hygrometer.

50. D

The stem root word joc- means relating to joke, for example jocularity.

Word List 3 – Most Common Prefix.

A prefix is a word part at the beginning of a word which helps create the meaning. Understanding prefix is a powerful tool for increasing your vocabulary because many prefix are used by two, three or more words. The word prefix contains a prefix "pre-," which means before. If you know the meaning of the prefix, you can guess the meaning of the word, even if you are not familiar with the word.

Prefix may have more than one meaning. Here is a list of 100 commonly used prefixes along with their meaning and an example of their use.

Study the list below and then answer 50 questions on common prefixes.

Prefix	Meaning	Example
a-, an-	without	amoral
ana-	out of	anachronism
ante-	before	antecedent
acro-	high up	Acropolis
anti-	against	antifreeze
ab-	away	abduction
auto-	self	autopilot
aero-	air	aeroplane
agro-	farming	agriculture
auto-	self	automatic
anti-	against	antidote
anthropo-	human	anthropology
aqua	water	aquarium
bathy-	deep	bathyscape
bio-	life	biology
baro-	atmosphere	barometer
brady-	slow	bradycardia
bi-	two	bicycle
broncho-	breathing	bronchitis
biblio-	relating to books	bibliophile
circum-	around	circumcision
cent- centi-	hundred	centenary

Prefix	Meaning	Example
counter-	against, opposite	counterpoint
cardio-	heart	cardiovascular
cyto-	hollow, receptacle,	cytoplasm
cosmo-		cosmology
cryo-	frost, icy cold	cryogenics
chrono-	time	chronology
com-, con-	together	conference
contra-, contro	against, opposite	contradiction, contraception
crypto-	hidden	cryptography
demo-	people, nation	demographics
dermo-, derma-	skin	dermatology
deci-	one tenth	deciliter
dis-	reverse	dissent
de-	taking away	decentralization
deca	ten	decameter
dynamo-	power, force	dynamic
eco-	house	economy
ectos-	outside	exoskeleton
ex-	out of, former	extract
extra-	more than	extracurricular
hydro	water	hydration
hyper-	over, more	hyperactive
homo-	same	homonym
hetero-	different	heterosexual
hydro	water	hydroplane
hemi	half	hemisphere
intra-	between	intravenous
im-, ir-, il-, in-,	not, without	illegal, inconsiderate,
inter-	between	intersect
in-	into	insert
intra	within	intramural, intranet
intro-	in, into	introspect
kilo-	thousand	kilogram
macro	large	marcoeconomics
meta-	after, beyond	metacarpal

Prefix	Meaning	Example
multi-	many	multimillionaire
mis-	bad, wrong	miscarriage
micro-	small, million	microscope, microgram
mega-, megal-	million, large	megabyte, megaphone
macro-	large	macroeconomics
micro-	one millionth	microgram
mal-	bad	maladjusted
mono-	one	monocle
mini-	small	miniskirt, miniscule
multi	many	multiple, multiplicity
non-	not	nonconformist
non-	not, without	nonentity
neo-	new	Neolithic
omni-	all, every	omniscient
over-	too much	overpopulation
octa	eight	octagon
pre-	before	preview , precedent
penta-	five	pentagon
post-	after	Post-Modern
pro-	in favour of	pro-choice, promotion
pan-	all	pantheon
poly-	many	polygon
quadr-, quart-	four	quadrangle
retro-	backward	retrospect
re-, red-	together	reconnect
re-	again, repeatedly	reflection, reduction
recti-	proper, straight	rectangle, rectify
sub-	under	submarine
semi-	half	semi-automatic , semi-detached
syn-	same time	synchronize
super-	extremely	superhuman
tachy-, tacho-	fast, speed	tachometer
tele-, telo-	long distance	telecommunications, telephoto
trans-	across, beyond	transubstantiation
thermo	heat	thermos
tri-	three	triangle, tricolor

Prefix	Meaning	Example
thermo	heat	thermometer
un-	not, opposite	unconstitutional
uni-	one, single	unification
ultra	beyond	ultraviolet
zoo-	relating to animals	zoology

Prefix Part I Answer Sheet.

1. (A) (B) (C) (D)   11. (A) (B) (C) (D)   21. (A) (B) (C) (D)

2. (A) (B) (C) (D)   12. (A) (B) (C) (D)   22. (A) (B) (C) (D)

3. (A) (B) (C) (D)   13. (A) (B) (C) (D)   23. (A) (B) (C) (D)

4. (A) (B) (C) (D)   14. (A) (B) (C) (D)   24. (A) (B) (C) (D)

5. (A) (B) (C) (D)   15. (A) (B) (C) (D)   25. (A) (B) (C) (D)

6. (A) (B) (C) (D)   16. (A) (B) (C) (D)

7. (A) (B) (C) (D)   17. (A) (B) (C) (D)

8. (A) (B) (C) (D)   18. (A) (B) (C) (D)

9. (A) (B) (C) (D)   19. (A) (B) (C) (D)

10. (A) (B) (C) (D)   20. (A) (B) (C) (D)

PREFIX PART II ANSWER SHEET.

1. (A) (B) (C) (D)   11. (A) (B) (C) (D)   21. (A) (B) (C) (D)

2. (A) (B) (C) (D)   12. (A) (B) (C) (D)   22. (A) (B) (C) (D)

3. (A) (B) (C) (D)   13. (A) (B) (C) (D)   23. (A) (B) (C) (D)

4. (A) (B) (C) (D)   14. (A) (B) (C) (D)   24. (A) (B) (C) (D)

5. (A) (B) (C) (D)   15. (A) (B) (C) (D)   25. (A) (B) (C) (D)

6. (A) (B) (C) (D)   16. (A) (B) (C) (D)

7. (A) (B) (C) (D)   17. (A) (B) (C) (D)

8. (A) (B) (C) (D)   18. (A) (B) (C) (D)

9. (A) (B) (C) (D)   19. (A) (B) (C) (D)

10. (A) (B) (C) (D)   20. (A) (B) (C) (D)

Prefix Questions Part I.

1. Choose the prefix that means single or uniform.

    a. Uni-

    b. Epic-

    c. Hydra-

    d. Si-

2. Choose the prefix that means self.

    a. Bi-

    b. Me-

    c. Auto-

    d. Co-

3. Choose the prefix that means half.

    a. Non-

    b. Gra-

    c. Dre-

    d. Hemi-

4. Choose the prefix that means long distance.

    a. Mini-

    b. Tele-

    c. Dis-

    d. Sci-

5. Choose the prefix that means ten.

    a. Deca-

    b. Tri-

    c. Ti-

    d. Bri-

6. Choose the prefix that means straight and proper.

    a. Ultra-

    b. Recti-

    c. Pan-

    d. De-

7. Choose the prefix that means water.

    a. Cent-

    b. Andr-

    c. Uni-

    d. Hydro-

8. Choose the prefix that means time.

    a. Trans-

    b. Inter-

    c. Chrono-

    d. Demo-

9. Choose the prefix that means bad.

    a. Bathy-

    b. Mal-

    c. Re-

    d. Ectos-

10. Choose the prefix that means five.

    a. Fi-

    b. Dynamo-

    c. Post-

    d. Penta-

11. Choose the prefix that means farming.

    a. Agro-

    b. Kilo-

    c. Poly-

    d. Contra-

12. Choose the prefix that means new.

    a. Andro-

    b. Acro-

    c. Neo-

    d. Mis-

13. Choose the prefix that means all or every.

    a. Multi-

    b. Omni-

    c. Creo-

    d. Mal-

14. Choose the prefix that means after.

    a. Post-

    b. Acro-

    c. Neo-

    d. Mis-

15. Choose the prefix that means cold.

    a. Ex-

    b. Zoo-

    c. Cryo-

    d. Fro-

16. Choose the prefix that means above.

    a. Trans-

    b. Gro-

    c. Epi-

    d. Brady-

17. Choose the prefix that means atmosphere.

    a. Baro-

    b. Cro-

    c. Po-

    d. Ato-

18. Choose the prefix that means at the same time.

    a. Semi-

    b. Syn-

    c. Meta-

    d. Omni-

19. Choose the prefix that means too much.

    a. Plu-

    b. Into-

    c. Nat-

    d. Over-

20. Choose the prefix that means opposite and against.

    a. Contra-

    b. Deg-

    c. Erg-

    d. Re-

21. Choose the prefix that means one millionth.

   a. Mil-

   b. Non-

   c. Micro-

   d. Con-

22. Choose the prefix that means wrong or bad.

   a. Dis-

   b. Demo-

   c. Grad-

   d. Mis-

23. Choose the prefix that means many.

   a. Poly-

   b. Pro-

   c. Pan-

   d. Recti-

24. Choose the prefix that means two.

   a. Tri-

   b. Bi-

   c. Maxi-

   d. Dre-

25. Choose the prefix that means before.

   a. Anti

   b. Tachy-

   c. Pre-

   d. Quin-

Prefix Questions Part I Answer Key.

1. A
The prefix uni means single and uniform, for example unification.

2. C
The prefix auto means self, for example automatic.

3. D
The prefix hemi means half, for example hemisphere.

4. B
The prefix tele means long distance, for example telecommunication.

5. A
The prefix deca means ten, for example decade.

6. B
The prefix recti means straight and proper, for example rectify.

7. D
The prefix hydro means water, for example hydroplane.

8. C
The prefix chrono means time, for example chronograph.

9. B
The prefix mal means bad, for example maladjusted.

10. D
The prefix penta means five, for example pentagon.

11. A
The prefix agro means farming, for example agronomy.

12. C
The prefix neo means new, for example Neolithic.

13. B
The prefix omni means all or every, for example omniscient.

14. A
The prefix post means after, for example postwar.

15. C
The prefix cryo means icy cold, for example cryogenics.

16. C
The prefix epi means above, for example epitaph.

17. A
The prefix baro means atmosphere, for example barometer.

18. B
The prefix syn means same time, for example synchronize.

19. D
The prefix over means too much, for example overtime.

20. A
The prefix contra means opposite or against, for example contradiction.

21. C
The prefix micro means one millionth, for example microgram.

22. D
The prefix mis means wrong or bad, for example misstep or miscarriage.

23. A
The prefix poly means many, for example polygon.

24. B
The prefix bi means two, for example bicycle.

25. C
The prefix pre means before, for example preview.

Prefix Questions Part II

1. Choose the best meaning of the prefix aqua.

   a. Water

   b. Past

   c. Change

   d. Extreme heat

2. Choose the best meaning of the prefix anti.

   a. Water

   b. Enemies

   c. Against

   d. Missing the mark

3. Choose the best meaning of the prefix bio.

   a. Study

   b. Bible

   c. Animals

   d. Life

4. Choose the best meaning of the prefix circum.

   a. Square shape

   b. Around

   c. Junior in level

   d. Border line

5. Choose the best meaning of the prefix ex.

   a. Excessive

   b. After

   c. Former

   d. Next

6. Choose the best meaning of the prefix thermo.

    a. Long distance

    b. Heat

    c. Hard

    d. Pressure

7. Choose the best meaning of the prefix intra.

    a. Square shape

    b. Between

    c. Round

    d. Border line

8. Choose the best meaning of the prefix kilo.

    a. Thousand

    b. Hundred

    c. Plenty

    d. Extra

9. Choose the best meaning of the prefix multi.

    a. Blood

    b. Severe pain

    c. Narrow

    d. Many

10. Choose the best meaning of the prefix mini.

    a. Harsh

    b. Acute

    c. Small

    d. Larger than normal

11. Choose the best meaning of the prefix octa.

    a. Extreme

    b. Eight

    c. Short

    d. Water animal

12. Choose the best meaning of the prefix pro.

    a. Extremely cold

    b. Before

    c. In favor of

    d. Repeat

13. Choose the best meaning of the prefix quad.

    a. 3-Sided

    b. Four

    c. Five

    d. Many sided

14. Choose the best meaning of the prefix retro.

    a. Related to temperature

    b. Against

    c. Deny

    d. Backward

15. Choose the best meaning of the prefix semi.

    a. Half

    b. Complete

    c. Related to money

    d. Related to weapons

16. Choose the best meaning of the prefix sub.

    a. Faster

    b. Smaller

    c. Under

    d. Related to water

17. Choose the best meaning of the prefix ultra.

    a. Double

    b. Far beyond

    c. Slow

    d. Related to health

18. Choose the best meaning of the prefix tri.

    a. Three

    b. Acrobat

    c. Related to time

    d. Related to air

19. Choose the best meaning of the prefix un.

    a. Alone

    b. Together

    c. Opposite

    d. Agreement

20. Choose the best meaning of the prefix zoo.

    a. Same time

    b. Relating to animals

    c. Related to the forest

    d. Large house

21. Choose the best meaning of the prefix ante.

    a. Relating to the heart

    b. Relating to food

    c. Male animals

    d. Before or previous

22. Choose the best meaning of the prefix homo.

    a. Same

    b. Red in color

    c. Related to blood

    d. Hard

23. Choose the best meaning of the prefix macro.

    a. Related to economy

    b. Different

    c. Large

    d. Female

PREFIX QUESTIONS PART II ANSWER KEY.

1. A
The prefix aqua means relating to water, for example, aquarium.

2. C
The prefix anti means against, for example, antichrist.

3. D
The prefix bio means life, for example, biology.

4. B
The prefix circum means around, for example circumference.

5. C
The prefix ex means former or out of, for example extract or ex-president

6. B
The prefix thermo means heat, for example thermostat.

7. B
The prefix intra means between, for example intravenous.

8. A
The prefix kilo means thousand, for example kilogram.

9. D
The prefix multi means many, for example multiple.

10. C
The prefix mini means small, for example miniscule.

11. B
The prefix octa means eight, for example octagon.

12. C
The prefix pro means in favor of, for example promotion.

13. B
The prefix quad means four, for example quadruped, or four

legs.

14. D
The prefix retro means backward, for example retrospect.

15. A
The prefix semi means half, for example semi-detached.

16. C
The prefix sub means under, for example submarine.

17. B
The prefix ultra means far beyond, for example ultraviolet.

18. A
The prefix tri means three, for example trilogy.

19. C
The prefix un means opposite and not, for example unconstitutional.

20. B
The prefix zoo means animal, for example zoology.

21. D
The prefix ante means before, for example antecedent.

22. A
The prefix homo means same, for example homosexual.

23. C
The prefix macro mean large, for example macroeconomics.

Word List 4 – Most Common Synonyms

Synonyms, like prefix and stem words are a great two-for-one strategy for improving your vocabulary fast. Below is a list of the most common synonyms followed by 30 questions.

Word	Synonym	Synonym
Amazing	Extraordinary	Astonishing
Aggravate	Infuriate	Annoy
Arrogant	Imperious	Disdainful
Answer	Respond	Reply
Antagonist	Enemy	Adversary
Attain	Achieve	Reach
Benevolence	Kindness	Charitable
Berate	Disapprove	Criticize
Beautiful	Gorgeous	Attractive
Big	Gigantic	Enormous
Boisterous	Loud	Rowdy
Boring	Uninteresting	Dull
Budget	Plan	Allot
Contradict	Oppose	Deny
Category	Division	Classification
Complete	Comprehensive	Total
Conspicuous	Prominent	Bold
Catch	Seize	Capture
Chubby	Fat	Plump
Congenial	Pleasant	Friendly
Criticize	Berate	Belittle
Delicious	Delectable	Appetizing
Describe	Portray	Picture
Destroy	Ruin	Wreck
Dwindle	Diminish	Abate
Difference	Contrast	Dissimilarity
Decay	Rot	Decompose
Decent	Pure	Honorable
Decipher	Decode	Decrypt
Eager	Enthusiastic	Willing
Elaborate	Enhance	Explain
Explain	Elaborate	Elucidate

Word	Synonym	Synonym
Enjoy	Relish	Savor
Estimate	Predict	Guess
Eccentric	Weird	Odd
Embezzle	Misappropriate	Steal
Fastidious	Exacting	Particular
Flatter	Praise	Compliment
Fantasy	Imagine	Day dream
Fondle	Caress	Stroke
Furious	Raging	Angry
Good	Sound	Excellent
Genuine	Real	Actual
Gay	Happy	Cheerful
Ghastly	Horrible	Gruesome
Handicap	Disadvantage	Disability
Haughty	Proud	Arrogant
Hypocrisy	Pretense	Duplicity
Humiliate	Shame	Humble
Impregnable	Unconquerable	Indomitable
Interesting	Captivating	Engaging
Illicit	Illegal	Unlawful
Immaterial	Irrelevant	Unimportant
Illustrious	Famous	Noble
Impregnable	Unconquerable	Unbeatable
Incoherent	Jumbled	Confused
Insidious	Deceitful	Duplicitous
Itinerary	Schedule	Route
Intrusive	Invasive	Nosy
Jargon	Slang	Lingo
Jovial	Jolly	Genial
Juvenile	Immature	Adolescent
Justification	Reason	Excuse
Justification	Scoff	Mock
Jostle	Shove	Push
Keep	Hold	Retain
Keen	Sharp	Acute
Keel	Swagger	Reel
Look	Gaze	Inspect
Little	Tiny	Small
Limitation	Constraint	Boundary
Least	Lowest	Minimum
Malice	Bitterness	Spite
Match	Identical	Correspond

Study >> Practice >> Succeed!   *Complete* Test Preparation

Word	Synonym	Synonym
Memorial	Commemorate	Monument
Meager	Bare	Scanty
Momento	Gift	Keepsake
Necessary	Required	Essential
Negotiate	Scheme	Bargain
Novice	Learner	Beginner
Narrate	Disclose	Tell
Negligible	Unimportant	Insignificant
Obstinate	Adamant	Stubborn
Omen	Premonition	Foreboding
Opulence	Abundance	Wealth
Omit	Exclude	Disregard
Perplex	Confuse	Astonish
Parcel	Bundle	Package
Pause	Wait	Break
Plight	Situation	Scenario
Quack	Fake	Charlatan
Quip	Joke	Jest
Renown	Famous	Popular
Radiate	Emanate	Effuse
Run	Accelerate	Dash
Romantic	Amorous	Loving
Rebel	Dissent	Renegade
Reconcile	Harmonize	Conciliate
Render	Give	Present
Sanction	Authorize	Approve
Satisfy	Sate	Gratify
Strong	Powerful	Hard
Sealed	Stroll	Walk
Shackle	Retrain	Confine
Saunter	Shut	Close
Terminate	End	Finish
True	Accurate	Factual
Thrive	Prosper	Progress
Tumult	Confusion	Disturbance
Tacit	Implicit	Implied
Terminate	End	Finish
Thaw	Unfreeze	Defrost
Update	Modernize	Renew
Ultimate	Supreme	Eventual
Uncanny	Mysterious	Spooky
Valid	Accurate	Legitimate

Study >> Practice >> Succeed!

Complete Test Preparation

Word	Synonym	Synonym
Verify	Validate	Certify
Vacate	Quit	Resign
Various	Assortment	Diverse
Wrath	Rage	Fury
Weird	Strange	Odd
Yearly	Annually	Year by year
Yank	Pull	Draw
Yearn	Long for	Desire
Zealous	Enthusiastic	Dedicated
Zoom	Speed off	Hurry

SYNONYM PRACTICE QUESTION ANSWER SHEET.

1. (A) (B) (C) (D)   11. (A) (B) (C) (D)   21. (A) (B) (C) (D)

2. (A) (B) (C) (D)   12. (A) (B) (C) (D)   22. (A) (B) (C) (D)

3. (A) (B) (C) (D)   13. (A) (B) (C) (D)   23. (A) (B) (C) (D)

4. (A) (B) (C) (D)   14. (A) (B) (C) (D)   24. (A) (B) (C) (D)

5. (A) (B) (C) (D)   15. (A) (B) (C) (D)   25. (A) (B) (C) (D)

6. (A) (B) (C) (D)   16. (A) (B) (C) (D)

7. (A) (B) (C) (D)   17. (A) (B) (C) (D)

8. (A) (B) (C) (D)   18. (A) (B) (C) (D)

9. (A) (B) (C) (D)   19. (A) (B) (C) (D)

10. (A) (B) (C) (D)   20. (A) (B) (C) (D)

Synonym Practice Questions.

1. Select the synonym of conspicuous.

   a. Important

   b. Prominent

   c. Beautiful

   d. Convincing

2. Select the synonym of benevolence.

   a. Happiness

   b. Courage

   c. Kindness

   d. Loyalty

3. Select the synonym of boisterous.

   a. Loud

   b. Soft

   c. Gentle

   d. Warm

4. Select the synonym of fondle.

   a. Hold

   b. Caress

   c. Throw

   d. Keep

5. Select the synonym of impregnable.

   a. Unconquerable

   b. Impossible

   c. Unlimited

   d. Imperfect

6. Select the synonym of antagonist.

   a. Supporter

   b. Fan

   c. Enemy

   d. Partner

7. Select the synonym of memento.

   a. Monument

   b. Remembrance

   c. Gift

   d. Idea

8. Select the synonym of insidious.

   a. Wise

   b. Brave

   c. Helpful

   d. Deceitful

9. Select the synonym of itinerary.

   a. Schedule

   b. Guidebook

   c. Pass

   d. Diary

10. Select the synonym of illustrious.

   a. Rich

   b. Noble

   c. Gallant

   d. Poor

11. Select the pair below that are synonyms.

a. Jargon and Slang

b. Slander and Plagiarism

c. Devotion and Devout

d. Current and Outdated

12. Select the pair below that are synonyms.

a. Render and Give

b. Recognition and Cognizant

c. Stem and Root

d. Adjust and Redo

13. Select the pair below that are synonyms.

a. Private and Public

b. Intrusive and Invasive

c. Mysterious and Unknown

d. Common and Unique

14. Select the pair below that are synonyms.

a. Renowned and Popular

b. Guard and Safe

c. Aggressive and Shy

d. Curtail and Avoid

15. Select the pair below that are synonyms.

a. Brevity and Ambiguous

b. Fury and Light-hearted

c. Incoherent and Jumbled

d. Benign And Malignant

16. Select the pair below that are synonyms.

    a. Congenial and Pleasant

    b. Distort and Similar

    c. Valuable and Rich

    d. Asset and Liability

17. Select the pair below that are synonyms.

    a. Circumstance and Plan

    b. Negotiate and Scheme

    c. Ardent and Whimsical

    d. Plight and Situation

18. Select the pair below that are synonyms.

    a. Berate and Criticize

    b. Unspoken and Unknown

    c. Tenet and Favor

    d. Turf and Seashore

19. Select the pair below that are synonyms.

    a. Adequate and Inadequate

    b. Sate and Satisfy

    c. Sufficient and Lacking

    d. Spectator and Teacher

20. Select the pair below that are synonyms.

    a. Pensive and Alibi

    b. Terminate and End

    c. Plot and Point

    d. Jaded and Honest

CHOOSE THE SYNONYM OF THE UNDERLINED WORD.

21. I cannot wait to try some of the <u>delectable</u> dishes served in the new restaurant.

    a. Unique

    b. Expensive

    c. New

    d. Delicious

22. Can you <u>describe</u> the character of Juliet in the play?

    a. Report

    b. Portray

    c. State

    d. Draw

23. The soldiers <u>destroyed</u> the rebel's camp.

    a. Ruined

    b. Ended

    c. Fixed

    d. Conquered

24. There is a big <u>difference</u> in Esther Pete's grades.

    a. Complication

    b. Dissimilarity

    c. Minus

    d. Increase

25. I can <u>attain</u> my goals in life when I study hard.

    a. Finish

    b. Forget

    c. Effect

    d. Achieve

26. The lecture was so <u>boring</u> everybody was starting to get sleepy.

    a. Uninteresting

    b. Sensible

    c. Fast

    d. Exciting

27. The <u>eager</u> crowd yelled and cheered for their favorite team during the basketball tournament.

    a. Bored

    b. Uninterested

    c. Angry

    d. Enthusiastic

28. The government is planning to <u>end</u> famine through mass food production.

    a. Close

    b. Avoid

    c. Stop

    d. Start

29. Children <u>enjoy</u> playing in the park with their playmates.

    a. Dislike

    b. Relish

    c. Spend

    d. Uninterested

30. Can you <u>elaborate</u> on the reason behind your tardiness?

    a. Define

    b. Correct

    c. Explain

    d. Interpret

SYNONYM PRACTICE ANSWER KEY

1. B
Conspicuous and prominent are synonyms.

2. C
Benevolence and kindness are synonyms.

3. A
Boisterous and loud are synonyms.

4. B
Fondle and caress are synonyms.

5. A
Impregnable and unconquerable are synonyms.

6. C
Antagonist and enemy are synonyms.

7. C
Memento and gift are synonyms.

8. D
Insidious and deceitful are synonyms.

9. A
Itinerary and schedule are synonyms.

10. B
Illustrious and noble are synonyms.

11. A
Jargon and slang are synonyms.

12. A
Render and give are synonyms.

13. B
Intrusive and invasive are synonyms.

14. A
Renowned and popular are synonyms.

15. C
Incoherent and jumbled are synonyms.

16. A
Congenial and pleasant are synonyms.

17. D
Plight and situation are synonyms.

18. A
Berate and criticize are synonyms.

19. B
Sate and satisfy are synonyms.

20. B
Terminate and end are synonyms.

21. D
Delectable and delicious are synonyms.

22. B
Describe and portray are synonyms.

23. A
Destroy and ruin are synonyms.

24. B
Difference and dissimilarity are synonyms.

25. D
Attain and achieve are synonyms.

26. A
Boring and uninteresting are synonyms.

27. D
Eager and enthusiastic are synonyms.

28. C
End and stop are synonyms.

29. B
Enjoy and relish are synonyms.

30. C
Elaborate and explain are synonyms.

Word List 5 – Most Common Antonyms.

Antonyms, like synonyms and stems, are a great two-for-one strategy for increasing your vocabulary. Below is a list of the most common antonyms, following by practice questions.

Word	Antonym	Antonym
Abundant	Scarce	Insufficient
Abnormal	Standard	Normal
Advance	Retreat	Recoil
Aimless	Directed	Motivated
Absurd	Sensible	Wise
Authentic	Imitation	Fake
Benevolence	Animosity	Indifference
Bloodless	Sensitive	Feeling
Blissful	Miserable	Sorrowful
Brilliant	Dulled	Dark
Certainty	Uncertainty	Doubtful
Capable	Inept	Incompetent
Cease	Begin	Commence
Charge	Discharge	Exonerate
Cohesive	Weak	Yielding
Console	Aggravate	Annoy
Confused	Enlightened	Attentive
Captivity	Liberty	Freedom
Diligent	Negligent	Languid
Dreadful	Pleasant	Pleasing
Decisive	Procrastinating	Indecisive
Deranged	Sane	Sensible
Disable	Enable	Assist
Discord	Harmony	Cooperation
Disjointed	Connected	Attached
Dogmatic	Flexible	Amenable
Erratic	Consistent	Dependable
Ecstatic	Despaired	Tormented
Eligible	Improper	Unfit
Escalate	Diminish	Decrease
Elusive	Confronting	Attracting
Exhibit	Conceal	Hide
Fidelity	Disloyalty	Infidelity

Word	Antonym	Antonym
Factual	Imprecise	Incorrect
Fearful	Courageous	Brave
Famous	Obscure	Unknown
Gaunt	Plump	Thick
Graceful	Awkward	Careless
Goodness	Meanness	Wickedness
Glamorous	Irritating	Offensive
Hard	Soft	Pliable
Hoarse	Smooth	Pleasing
Hidden	Bare	Exposed
Hearty	Apathetic	Lethargic
Harmful	Harmless	Safe
Harsh	Mild	Gentle
Hero	Villain	Antagonist
Idiotic	Smart	Intelligent
Idle	Busy	Working
Illegal	Lawful	Authorized
Illicit	Legal	Lawful
Illuminate	Obfuscate	Confuse
Immense	Tiny	Small
Intimate	Formal	Unfriendly
Identical	Opposite	Different
Immense	Minute	Tiny
Justice	Lawlessness	Unfairness
Jealous	Content	Trusting
Joyful	Sorrowful	Sad
Jumpy	Composed	Collected
Knack	Inability	Ineptitude
Kill	Create	Bear
Keen	Uninterested	Reluctant
Laughable	Serious	Grave
Latter	Former	First
Legible	Unreadable	Unclear
Literal	Figurative	Metaphorical
Loathe	Love	Like
Legendary	Factual	True
Large	Little	Small
Miserable	Cheerful	Joyful
Moderate	Excessive	Unrestrained
Magical	Boring	Ordinary
Minor	Major	Significant
Myriad	Few	Scant

Complete Test Preparation

Word	Antonym	Antonym
Narrow	Broad	Wide
Nasty	Pleasant	Magnificent
Nimble	Awkward	Clumsy
Nutritious	Unhealthy	Unwholesome
Optional	Compulsory	Required
Operational	Inactive	Inoperative
Optimistic	Pessimistic	Doubtful
Ordinary	Abnormal	Uncommon
Pester	Delight	Please
Penalize	Forgive	Reward
Placate	Agitate	Upset
Practical	Unfeasible	Unrealistic
Pensive	Shallow	Ignorant
Queasy	Comfortable	Satisfied
Quietly	Loudly	Audibly
Quirky	Conventional	Normal
Qualified	Unqualified	Incapable
Rapid	Slow	Leisurely
Refuse	Agree	Assent
Reluctant	Enthusiastic	Excited
Romantic	Realistic	Pragmatic
Ridicule	Flatter	Praise
Refresh	Damage	Ruin
Rough	Level	Smooth
Sacrifice	Refuse	Hold
Sadistic	Humane	Kind
Sane	Deranged	Insane
Save	Spend	Splurge
Scarce	Abundant	Plenty
Scorn	Approve	Delight
Scatter	Gather	Collect
Shrink	Expand	Grow
Simple	Complex	Complicated
Stingy	Generous	Bountiful
Sterile	Dirty	Infected
Tedious	Interesting	Exciting
Tactful	Indiscreet	Careless
Tough	Weak	Vulnerable
Transparent	Opaque	Cloudy
Terminate	Initiate	Start
Truth	Lie	Untruth
Understand	Misunderstand	Misinterpret

Word	Antonym	Antonym
Usable	Useless	Unfit
Validate	Veto	Reject
Vanquish	Endorse	Surrender
Vanish	Appear	Materialize
Vicious	Gentle	Nice
Vice	Virtue	Propriety
Villain	Hero	Savior
Vulnerable	Strong	Powerful
Wary	Reckless	Careless
Wasteful	Frugal	Thrifty
Wane	Grow	Increase
Weary	Lively	Energetic
Young	Old	Mature
Yonder	Nearby	Close
Zealous	Lethargic	Unenthusias-tic
Zap	Inactive	Dull

ANTONYM PRACTICE ANSWER SHEET

1. Ⓐ Ⓑ Ⓒ Ⓓ   11. Ⓐ Ⓑ Ⓒ Ⓓ   21. Ⓐ Ⓑ Ⓒ Ⓓ

2. Ⓐ Ⓑ Ⓒ Ⓓ   12. Ⓐ Ⓑ Ⓒ Ⓓ   22. Ⓐ Ⓑ Ⓒ Ⓓ

3. Ⓐ Ⓑ Ⓒ Ⓓ   13. Ⓐ Ⓑ Ⓒ Ⓓ   23. Ⓐ Ⓑ Ⓒ Ⓓ

4. Ⓐ Ⓑ Ⓒ Ⓓ   14. Ⓐ Ⓑ Ⓒ Ⓓ   24. Ⓐ Ⓑ Ⓒ Ⓓ

5. Ⓐ Ⓑ Ⓒ Ⓓ   15. Ⓐ Ⓑ Ⓒ Ⓓ   25. Ⓐ Ⓑ Ⓒ Ⓓ

6. Ⓐ Ⓑ Ⓒ Ⓓ   16. Ⓐ Ⓑ Ⓒ Ⓓ   26. Ⓐ Ⓑ Ⓒ Ⓓ

7. Ⓐ Ⓑ Ⓒ Ⓓ   17. Ⓐ Ⓑ Ⓒ Ⓓ   27. Ⓐ Ⓑ Ⓒ Ⓓ

8. Ⓐ Ⓑ Ⓒ Ⓓ   18. Ⓐ Ⓑ Ⓒ Ⓓ   28. Ⓐ Ⓑ Ⓒ Ⓓ

9. Ⓐ Ⓑ Ⓒ Ⓓ   19. Ⓐ Ⓑ Ⓒ Ⓓ   29. Ⓐ Ⓑ Ⓒ Ⓓ

10. Ⓐ Ⓑ Ⓒ Ⓓ   20. Ⓐ Ⓑ Ⓒ Ⓓ   30. Ⓐ Ⓑ Ⓒ Ⓓ

Antonym Practice Questions

1. Choose the antonym pair.

   a. Abundant and Scarce

   b. Several and Plenty

   c. Analysis and Review

   d. Obtrusive and Hierarchical

2. Choose the antonym pair.

   a. Bully and Animal

   b. Teary-eyed and Gentle

   c. Tough and Weak

   d. Strong and Massive

3. Choose the antonym pair.

   a. Illuminate and Obfuscate

   b. Resonance and Significance

   c. Resonate and Justify

   d. Rationalize and Practice

4. Choose the antonym pair.

   a. Simple and Complex

   b. Plain and Plaid

   c. Shy and Sinister

   d. Vibrant and Cheery

5. Choose the antonym pair.

   a. Elevate and Escalate

   b. Exhibit and Conceal

   c. Boast and Brood

   d. Show and Contest

Study >> Practice >> Succeed!

Complete Test Preparation

6. Choose the antonym pair.

    a. Strict and Tight

    b. Hurtful and Offensive

    c. Unpleasant and Mean

    d. Stingy and Generous

7. Choose the antonym pair.

    a. New and Torn

    b. Advance and Retreat

    c. Next and Last

    d. Followed and Continued

8. Choose the antonym pair.

    a. Halt and Speed

    b. Began and Amidst

    c. Stop and Delay

    d. Cease and Begin

9. Choose the antonym pair.

    a. Scary and Horrific

    b. Honor and Justice

    c. Immense and Tiny

    d. Vague and Loud

10. Choose the antonym pair.

    a. Dissatisfied and Unsatisfied

    b. Disentangle and Acknowledge

    c. Discord and Harmony

    d. Fruition and Fusion

11. Choose the antonym pair.

    a. Late and Later

    b. Latter and Former

    c. Structure and Organization

    d. Latter and Rushed

12. Choose the antonym pair.

    a. Belittle and Bemuse

    b. Shrunk and Minimal

    c. Shrink and Expand

    d. Smelly and Odor

13. Choose the antonym pair.

    a. Repulsive and Repentant

    b. Reluctant and Enthusiastic

    c. Prepare and Ready

    d. Release and Give

14. Choose the antonym pair.

    a. Sovereign and Autonomy

    b. Disdain and Contempt

    c. Disorder and Disarray

    d. Refuse and Agree

15. Choose the antonym pair.

    a. Gentle and Soft

    b. Fragile and Breakable

    c. Vulnerable and Strong

    d. Vain and Tidy

16. Select the antonym of authentic.

   a. Real

   b. Imitation

   c. Apparition

   d. Dream

17. Select the antonym of villain.

   a. Actor

   b. Actress

   c. Heroine

   d. Hero

18. Select the antonym of vanish.

   a. Appear

   b. Lose

   c. Reflection

   d. Empty

19. Select the antonym of literal.

   a. Manuscript

   b. Writing

   c. Figurative

   d. Untrue

20. Select the antonym of harsh.

   a. Mild

   b. Light

   c. Bulky

   d. Bothersome

21. Select the antonym of splurge.

    a. Spend

    b. Count

    c. Use

    d. Save

22. Select the antonym of idle.

    a. Occupied

    b. Vacant

    c. Busy

    d. Interested

23. Select the antonym of console.

    a. Aggravate

    b. Empathize

    c. Sympathize

    d. Cry

24. Select the antonym of deranged.

    a. Chaos

    b. Dirty

    c. Bleak

    d. Sane

25. Select the antonym of disjointed.

    a. Connected

    b. Dismayed

    c. Recognized

    d. Bountiful

26. Select the antonym of confused.

   a. Frustrated

   b. Ashamed

   c. Enlightened

   d. Unknown

27. Select the antonym of benevolent.

   a. Nice

   b. Mature

   c. Honest

   d. Indifferent

28. Select the antonym of illicit.

   a. Unlawful

   b. Legal

   c. Anonymous

   d. Deceitful

29. Select the antonym of sterile.

   a. Dirty

   b. Alcoholic

   c. Drunk

   d. Drug

30. Select the antonym of myriad.

   a. Many

   b. Several

   c. Few

   d. Plenty

Antonyms Answer Key

1. A
Abundant and scarce are antonyms.

2. C
Tough and weak are antonyms.

3. A
Illuminate and obfuscate are antonyms.

4. A
Simple and complex are antonyms.

5. B
Exhibit and conceal are antonyms.

6. D
Stingy and generous are antonyms.

7. B
Advance and retreat are antonyms.

8. D
Cease and begin are antonyms.

9. C
Immense and tiny are antonyms.

10. C
Discord and harmony are antonyms.

11. B
Latter and former are antonyms.

12. C
Shrink and expand are antonyms.

13. B
Reluctant and enthusiastic are antonyms.

14. D
Refuse and agree are antonyms.

15. C
Vulnerable and strong are antonyms.

16. B
Authentic and imitation are antonyms.

17. D
Villain and hero are antonyms.

18. A
Vanish and appear are antonyms.

19. C
Literal and figurative are antonyms.

20. A
Harsh and mild are antonyms.

21. D
Splurge and save are antonyms.

22. C
Idle and busy are antonyms.

23. A
Console and aggravate are antonyms.

24. D
Deranged and sane are antonyms.

25. A
Disjointed and connected are antonyms.

26. C
Confused and enlightened are antonyms.

27. D
Benevolent and indifferent are antonyms.

28. B
Illicit and legal are antonyms.

29. A
Sterile and dirty are antonyms.

30. C
Myriad and few are antonyms.

How to Prepare for a Test

MOST STUDENTS HIDE THEIR HEADS AND PROCRASTINATE WHEN FACED WITH PREPARING FOR AN EXAMINATION, HOPING THAT SOMEHOW THEY WILL BE SPARED THE AGONY OF TAKING THAT TEST, ESPECIALLY IF IT IS A BIG ONE THAT THEIR FUTURES RELY ON. Avoiding the all-important test is what many students do best and unfortunately, they suffer the consequences because of their lack of preparation.

Test preparation requires strategy. It also requires a dedication to getting the job done. It is the perfect training ground for anyone planning a professional life. In addition to having a number of reliable strategies, the wise student also has a clear goal in mind and knows how to accomplish it. These tried and true concepts have worked well and will make your test preparation easier.

The Study Approach.

Take responsibility for your own test preparation.

It is a common- but big - mistake to link your studying to someone else's. Study partners are great, but only if they are reliable. It is your job to be prepared for the test, even if a study partner fails you. Do not allow others to distract you from your goals.

Prioritize the time available to study.

When do you learn best, early in the day or in the dark of night? Does your mind absorb and retain information most efficiently in small blocks of time, or do you require long stretches to get the most done? It is important to figure out the best blocks of time available to you when you can be the most productive. Try to consolidate activities to allow for longer periods of study time.

Find a quiet place where you will not be disturbed.

Do not try to squeeze in quality study time in any old location. Find someplace peaceful and with a minimum of distractions, such as the library, a park or even the laundry room. Good lighting is essential and you need to have comfortable seating and a desk surface large enough to hold your materials. It is probably not a great idea to study in your bedroom. You might be distracted by clothes on the floor, a book you have been planning to read, the telephone or something else. Besides, in the middle of studying, that bed will start to look very comfortable. Whatever you do, avoid using the bed as a place to study since you might fall asleep as a way of avoiding your work! That is the last thing you should be doing during study time.

The exception is flashcards. By far the most productive study time is sitting down and studying and studying only. However, with flashcards you can carry them with you and make use of odd moments, like standing in line or waiting for the bus. This isn't as productive, but it really helps and is definitely worth doing.

Determine what you need in order to study.

Gather together your books, your notes, your laptop and any other materials needed to focus on your study for this exam. Ensure you have everything you need so you don't waste time. Remember paper, pencils and erasers, sticky notes, bottled water and a snack. Keep your phone with you in case you need it to find out essential information, but keep it turned off so others can't distract you.

Have a positive attitude.

It is essential that you approach your studies for the test with an attitude that says you will pass it. And pass it with flying colors! This is one of the most important keys to successful study strategy. Believing that you are capable actually helps you to become capable.

THE STRATEGY OF STUDYING

Make materials easy to review and access.

Consolidate materials to help keep your study area clutter free. If you have a laptop and a means of getting on line, you do not need a dictionary and thesaurus as well since those things are easily accessible via the internet. Go through written notes and consolidate those, as well. Have everything you need, but do not weigh yourself down with duplicates.

Review class notes.

Stay on top of class notes and assignments by reviewing them frequently. Re-writing notes can be a terrific study trick, as it helps lock in information. Pay special attention to any comments that have been made by the teacher. If a study guide has been made available as part of the class materials, use it! It will be a valuable tool to use for studying.

Estimate how much time you will need.

If you are concerned about the amount of time you have available it is a good idea to set up a schedule so that you do not get bogged down on one section and end up without enough time left to study other things. Remember to schedule break time, and use that time for a little exercise or other stress reducing techniques.

Test yourself to determine your weaknesses.

Look online for additional assessment and evaluation tools available for a particular subject. Once you have determined areas of concern, you will be able to focus on studying the information they contain and just brush up on the other areas of the exam.

Study >> Practice >> Succeed!  *Complete* Test Preparation

Mental Prep – How to Psych Yourself Up for a Test

Because tests contribute mightily to your final class grade or to whether you are accepted into a program, it is understandable that taking tests can create a great deal of anxiety for many students. Even students who know they have learned all of the required material find their minds going blank as they stare at the words in the questions. One of the easiest ways to overcome that anxiety is to prepare mentally for the test. Mentally preparing for an exam is really not difficult. There are simple techniques that any student can learn to increase their chances of earning a great score on the day of the test.

Do not procrastinate.

Study the material for the test when it becomes available, and continue to review the material up until the test day. By waiting until the last minute and trying to cram for the test the night before, you actually increase the amount of anxiety you feel. This leads to an increase in negative self-talk. Telling yourself "I can't learn this. I am going to fail" is a pretty sure indication that you are right. At best, your performance on the test will not be as strong if you have procrastinated instead of studying.

Positive self-talk.

Positive self-talk serves both to drown out negative self-talk and to increase your confidence in your abilities. Whenever you begin feeling overwhelmed or anxious about the test, remind yourself that you have studied enough, you know the material and that you will pass the test. Use only positive words. Both negative and positive self-talk are really just your fantasy, so why not choose to be a winner?

Do not compare yourself to anyone else.

Do not compare yourself to other students, or your performance to theirs. Instead, focus on your own strengths and weaknesses and prepare accordingly. Regardless of how others perform, your performance is the only one that matters to your grade. Comparing yourself to others increases your anxiety and your level of negative self-talk before the test.

Visualize.

Make a mental image of yourself taking the test. You know the answers and feel relaxed. Visualize doing well on the test and having no problems with the material. Visualizations can increase your confidence and decrease the anxiety you might otherwise feel before the test. Instead of thinking of this as a test, see it as an opportunity to demonstrate what you have learned!

Avoid negativity.

Worry is contagious and viral - once it gets started it builds on itself. Cut it off before it gets to be a problem. Even if you are relaxed and confident, being around anxious, worried classmates might cause you to start feeling anxious. Before the test, tune out the fears of classmates. Feeling anxious and worried before an exam is normal, and every student experiences those feelings at some point. But you cannot allow these feelings to interfere with your ability to perform well. Practicing mental preparation techniques and remembering that the test is not the only measure of your academic performance will ease your anxiety and ensure that you perform at your best.

How to Take a Test

E VERYONE KNOWS THAT TAKING AN EXAM IS STRESSFUL, BUT IT DOES NOT HAVE TO BE THAT BAD! There are a few simple things that you can do to increase your score on any type of test. Take a look at these tips and consider how you can incorporate them into your study time.

How to Take a Test - The Basics.

Some tests are designed to assess your ability to quickly grab the necessary information; this type of exam makes speed a priority. Others are more concerned with your depth of knowledge, and how accurate it is. When you receive a test, look it over to determine whether the test is for speed or accuracy. If the test is for speed, like many standardized tests, your strategy is clear; answer as many questions as quickly as possible.

Watch out, though! There are a few tests that are designed to determine how fully and accurately you can answer the questions. Guessing on this type of test is a big mistake, because the teacher expects any student with an average grade to be able to complete the test in the time given. Racing through the test and making guesses that prove to be incorrect will cost you big time!

Every little bit helps.

If you are permitted calculators, or other materials, make sure you bring them, even if you do not think you will need them. Use everything at your disposal to increase your score.

Make time your friend.

Budget your time from the moment your pencil hits the page until you are finished with the exam, and stick to it! Virtually all standardized tests have a time limit for each section. The amount of time you are permitted for each portion of the test will almost certainly be included in the instructions or printed at the top of the page. If for some reason it is not immediately visible, rather than wasting your time hunting for it you can use the points or percentage of the score as a proxy to make an educated guess regarding the time limit.

Use the allotted time for each section and then move on to the next section whether you have completed the first section or not. Stick with the instructions and you will be able to answer the majority of the questions in each section.

With speed tests you may not be able to complete the entire test. Rest assured that you are not really expected to! The goal of this type of examination is to determine how quickly you can reach into your brain and access a particular piece of information, which is one way of determining how well you know it. If you know a test you are taking is a speed test, you will know the strategies to use for the best results.

Read the directions carefully.

Spend a few minutes reading the directions carefully before starting each section. Studies show students who read the instructions get higher marks! If you just glance at them, you may misunderstand and could blow the whole thing. Very small changes in the wording of the instructions or the punctuation can change the meaning completely. Do not make assumptions. Just because the directions are written one way in one section does not mean they will be exactly the same in all sections. Focus your attention and read what the instructions actually say, not what you think they are saying.

When reading the directions, underline the important parts. For example, if you are directed to circle the best answer, underline "circle" and "best". This flags the key concepts and will keep you focused.

If the exam is given with an answer booklet, copy the instructions to the top of the first page in the booklet. For complicated instructions, divide the directions into smaller steps and number each part.

Easy does it.

One smart way to tackle a test is to locate the easy questions and answer those first. This is a time-tested strategy that never fails, because it saves you a lot of unnecessary fretting. First, read the question and decide if you can answer it in less than a minute. If so, complete the question and go on to the next one. If not, skip it for now and continue on to the next question. By the time you have completed the first pass through this section of the exam, you will have answered a good number of questions. Not only does it boost your confidence, relieve anxiety and kick your memory up a notch, you will know exactly how many questions remain and can allot the rest of your time accordingly. Think of doing the easy questions first as a warm-up!

If you run out of time before you manage to tackle all the difficult questions, do not let it throw you. All that means is you have used your time in the most efficient way possible by answering as many questions correctly as you could. Missing a few points by not answering a question whose answer you do not know just means you spent that time answering one whose answer you did.

A word to the wise: Skipping questions for which you are drawing a complete blank is one thing, but we are not suggesting you skip every question you come across that you are not 100 % certain of. A good rule of thumb is to try to answer at least eight of every 10 questions the first time through.

Do not watch your watch.

At best, taking an important exam is an uncomfortable situation. If you are like most people, you might be tempted to subconsciously distract yourself from the task at hand. One of the most common ways to do so is by becoming obsessed with your watch or the wall clock. Do not watch your watch! Take it off and place it on the top corner of your desk, far enough away that you will not be tempted to look at it every two minutes. Better still, turn the watch face away from you. That way, every time you try to sneak a peek, you will be reminded to refocus your attention to the task at hand. Give yourself permission to check your watch or the wall clock af-

ter you complete each section. If you know yourself to be a bit of a slow-poke in other aspects of life, you can check your watch a bit more often. Even so, focus on answering the questions, not on how many minutes have elapsed since you last looked at it.

Divide and conquer.

What should you do when you come across a question that is so complicated you may not even be certain what is being asked? As we have suggested, the first time through the section you are best off skipping the question. But at some point, you will need to return to it and get it under control. The best way to handle questions that leave you feeling so anxious you can hardly think is by breaking them into manageable pieces. Solving smaller bits is always easier. For complicated questions, divide them into bite-sized pieces and solve these smaller sets separately. Once you understand what the reduced sections are really saying, it will be much easier to put them together and get a handle on the bigger question.

Reason your way through the toughest questions.

If you find that a question is so dense you can't figure out how to break it into smaller pieces, there are a few strategies that might help. First, read the question again and look for hints. Can you re-word the question in one or more different ways? This may give you clues. Look for words that can function as either verbs or nouns, and try to figure out from the sentence structure which it is in this case. Remember that many nouns in English have a number of different meanings. While some of those meanings might be related, in some cases they are completely distinct. If reading the sentence one way does not make sense, consider a different definition or meaning for a key word.

The truth is, it is not always necessary to understand a question to arrive at a correct answer! A trick that successful students understand is using Strategy 5, Elimination. In many cases, at least one answer is clearly wrong and can be crossed off of the list of possible correct answers. Next, look at the remaining answers and eliminate any that are only partially

true. You may still have to flat-out guess from time to time, but using the process of elimination will help you make your way to the correct answer more often than not - even when you don't know what the question means!

Do not leave early.

Use all the time allotted to you, even if you can't wait to get out of the testing room. Instead, once you have finished, spend the remaining time reviewing your answers. Go back to those questions that were most difficult for you and review your response. Another good way to use this time is to return to multiple choice questions in which you filled in a bubble. Do a spot check, reviewing every fifth or sixth question to make sure your answer coincides with the bubble you filled in. This is a great way to catch yourself if you made a mistake, skipped a bubble and therefore put all your answers in the wrong bubbles!

Become a super sleuth and look for careless errors. Look for questions that have double negatives or other odd phrasing; they might be an attempt to throw you off. Careless errors on your part might be the result of skimming a question and missing a key word. Words such as "always", "never", "sometimes" , "rarely" and the like can give a strong indication of the answer the question is really seeking. Don't throw away points by being careless!

Just as you budgeted time at the beginning of the test to allow for easy and more difficult questions, be sure to budget sufficient time to review your answers. On essay questions and math questions where you are required to show your work, check your writing to make sure it is legible.

Math questions can be especially tricky. The best way to double check math questions is by figuring the answer using a different method, if possible.

Here is another terrific tip. It is likely that no matter how hard you try, you will have a handful of questions you just are not sure of. Keep them in mind as you read through the rest of the test. If you can't answer a question, looking back over the test to find a different question that addresses the same topic

might give you clues.

We know that taking the test has been stressful and you can hardly wait to escape. Just keep in mind that leaving before you double-check as much as possible can be a quick trip to disaster. Taking a few extra minutes can make the difference between getting a bad grade and a great one. Besides, there will be lots of time to relax and celebrate after the test is turned in.

In the Test Room – What you MUST do!

If you are like the rest of the world, there is almost nothing you would rather avoid than taking a test. Unfortunately, that is not an option if you want to pass. Rather than suffer, consider a few attitude adjustments that might turn the experience from a horrible one to...well, an interesting one! Take a look at these tips. Simply changing how you perceive the experience can change the experience itself.

Get in the mood.

After weeks of studying, the big day has finally arrived. The worst thing you can do to yourself is arrive at the test site feeling frustrated, worried, and anxious. Keep a check on your emotional state. If your emotions are shaky before a test it can determine how well you do on the test. It is extremely important that you pump yourself up, believe in yourself, and use that confidence to get in the mood!

Don't fight reality.

Oftentimes, students resent tests, and with good reason. After all, many people do not test well, and they know the grade they end up with does not accurately reflect their true knowledge. It is easy to feel resentful because tests classify students and create categories that just don't seem fair. Face it: Students who are great at rote memorization and not that

good at actually analyzing material often score higher than those who might be more creative thinkers and balk at simply memorizing cold, hard facts. It may not be fair, but there it is anyway. Conformity is an asset on tests, and creativity is often a liability. There is no point in wasting time or energy being upset about this reality. Your first step is to accept the reality and get used to it. You will get higher marks when you realize tests do count and that you must give them your best effort. Think about your future and the career that is easier to achieve if you have consistently earned high grades. Avoid negative energy and focus on anything that lifts your enthusiasm and increases your motivation.

Get there early enough to relax.

If you are wound up, tense, scared, anxious, or feeling rushed, it will cost you. Get to the exam room early and relax before you go in. This way, when the exam starts, you are comfortable and ready to apply yourself. Of course, you do not want to arrive so early that you are the only one there. That will not help you relax; it will only give you too much time to sit there, worry and get wound up all over again.

If you can, visit the room in which you will be taking your exam a few days ahead of time. Have a visual image of the room can be surprisingly calming, because it takes away one of the big 'unknowns'. Not only that, but once you have visited, you know how to get there and will not be worried about getting lost. Furthermore, driving to the test site once lets you know how much time you need to allow for the trip. That means three potential stressors have been eliminated all at once.

Get it down on paper.

One of the advantages of arriving early is that it allows you time to recreate notes. If you spend a lot of time worrying about whether you will be able to remember information like names, dates, places, and mathematical formulas, there is a solution for that. Unless the exam you are taking allows you to use your books and notes, (and very few do) you will have to rely on memory. Arriving early gives to time to tap into your

memory and jot down key pieces of information you know will be asked. Just make certain you are allowed to make notes once you are in the testing site; not all locations will permit it. Once you get your test, on a small piece of paper write down everything you are afraid you will forget. It will take a minute or two but by dumping your worries onto the page you have effectively eliminated a certain amount of anxiety and driven off the panic you feel.

Get comfortable in your chair.

Here is a clever technique that releases physical stress and helps you get comfortable, even relaxed in your body. You will tense and hold each of your muscles for just a few seconds. The trick is, you must tense them hard for the technique to work. You might want to practice this technique a few times at home; you do not want an unfamiliar technique to add to your stress just before a test, after all! Once you are at the test site, this exercise can always be done in the rest room or another quiet location.

Start with the muscles in your face then work down your body. Tense, squeeze and hold the muscles for a moment or two. Notice the feel of every muscle as you go down your body. Scowl to tense your forehead, pull in your chin to tense your neck. Squeeze your shoulders down to tense your back. Pull in your stomach all the way back to your ribs, make your lower back tight then stretch your fingers. Tense your leg muscles and calves then stretch your feet and your toes. You should be as stiff as a board throughout your entire body.

Now relax your muscles in reverse starting with your toes. Notice how all the muscles feel as you relax them one by one. Once you have released a muscle or set of muscles, allow them to remain relaxed as you proceed up your body. Focus on how you are feeling as all the tension leaves. Start breathing deeply when you get to your chest muscles. By the time you have found your chair, you will be so relaxed it will feel like bliss!

Fight distraction.

A lucky few are able to focus deeply when taking an important examination, but most people are easily distracted, probably because they would rather be anyplace else! There are a number of things you can do to protect yourself from distraction.

Stay away from windows. If you select a seat near a window you may end up gazing out at the landscape instead of paying attention to the work at hand. Furthermore, any sign of human activity, from a single individual walking by to a couple having an argument or exchanging a kiss will draw your attention away from your important work. What goes on outside should not be allowed to distract you.

Choose a seat away from the aisle so you do not become distracted by people who leave early. People who leave the exam room early are often the ones who fail. Do not compare your time to theirs.

Of course you love your friends; that's why they are your friends! In the test room, however, they should become complete strangers inside your mind. Forget they are there. The first step is to physically distance yourself from friends or classmates. That way, you will not be tempted to glance at them to see how they are doing, and there will be no chance of eye contact that could either distract you or even lead to an accusation of cheating. Furthermore, if they are feeling stressed because they did not spend the focused time studying that you did, their anxiety is less likely to permeate your hard-earned calm.

Of course, you will want to choose a seat where there is sufficient light. Nothing is worse than trying to take an important examination under flickering lights or dim bulbs.

Ask the instructor or exam proctor to close the door if there is a lot of noise outside. If the instructor or proctor is unable to do so, block out the noise as best you can. Do not let anything disturb you.

Make sure you have enough pencils, pens and whatever else you will need. Many entrance exams do not permit you to bring personal items such as candy bars into the testing room. If this is the case with the exam you are sitting for, be sure to eat a nutritionally balanced breakfast. Eat protein, complex carbohydrates and a little fat to keep you feeling full and to supercharge your energy. Nothing is worse than a sudden drop in blood sugar during an exam.

Do not allow yourself to become distracted by being too cold or hot. Regardless of the weather outside, carry a sweater, scarf or jacket in case the air conditioning at the test site is set too high, or the heat set too low. By the same token, dress in layers so that you are prepared for a range of temperatures.

Bring a watch so that you can keep track of time management. The danger here is many students become obsessed with how many minutes have passed since the last question. Instead of wearing the watch, remove it and place it in the far upper corner of the desk with the face turned away. That way, you cannot become distracted by repeatedly glancing at the time, but it is available if you need to know it.

Drinking a gallon of coffee or gulping a few energy drinks might seem like a great idea, but it is, in fact, a very bad one. Caffeine, pep pills or other artificial sources of energy are more likely to leave you feeling rushed and ragged. Your brain might be clicking along, all right, but chances are good it is not clicking along on the right track! Furthermore, drinking lots of coffee or energy drinks will mean frequent trips to the rest room. This will cut into the time you should be spending answering questions and is a distraction in itself, since each time you need to leave the room you lose focus. Pep pills will only make it harder for you to think straight when solving complicated problems on the exam.

At the same time, if anxiety is your problem try to find ways around using tranquilizers during test-taking time. Even medically prescribed anti-anxiety medication can make you less alert and even decrease your motivation. Being motivated is what you need to get you through an exam. If your anxiety is so bad that it threatens to interfere with your ability to take an exam, speak to your doctor and ask for documentation. Many testing sites will allow non-distracting test rooms, extended testing time and other accommodations as long as a doctor's note that explains the situation is made available.

Keep Breathing.

It might not make a lot of sense, but when people become anxious, tense, or scared, their breathing becomes shallow and, in some cases, they stop breathing all together! Pay attention to your emotions, and when you are feeling worried, focus on your breathing. Take a moment to remind yourself to breathe deeply and regularly. Drawing in steady, deep breaths energizes the body. When you continue to breathe deeply you will notice you exhale all the tension.

It is a smart idea to rehearse breathing at home. With continued practice of this relaxation technique, you will begin to know the muscles that tense up under pressure. Call these your "signal muscles." These are the ones that will speak to you first, begging you to relax. Take the time to listen to those muscles and do as they ask. With just a little breathing practice, you will get into the habit of checking yourself regularly and when you realize you are tense, relaxation will become second nature.

AVOID ANXIETY PRIOR TO A TEST

Manage your time effectively.

This is a key to your success! You need blocks of uninterrupted time to study all the pertinent material. Creating and maintaining a schedule will help keep you on track, and will remind family members and friends that you are not available. Under no circumstances should you change your blocks of study time to accommodate someone else, or cancel a study session in order to do something more fun. Do not interfere with your study time for any reason!

Relax.

Use whatever works best for you to relieve stress. Some folks like a good, calming stretch with yoga, others find expressing themselves through journaling to be useful. Some hit the floor for a series of crunches or planks, and still others take a slow stroll around the garden. Integrate a little relaxation time into your schedule, and treat that time, too, as sacred.

Eat healthy.

Instead of reaching for the chips and chocolate, fresh fruits and vegetables are not only yummy but offer nutritional benefits that help to relieve stress. Some foods accelerate stress instead of reducing it and should be avoided. Foods that add to higher anxiety include artificial sweeteners, candy and other sugary foods, carbonated sodas, chips, chocolate, eggs, fried foods, junk foods, processed foods, red meat, and other foods containing preservatives or heavy spices. Instead, eat a bowl of berries and some yogurt!

Get plenty of ZZZZZZZs.

Do not cram or try to do an all-nighter. If you created a study schedule at the beginning, and if you have stuck with that schedule, have confidence! Staying up too late trying to cram in last-minute bits of information is going to leave you exhausted the next day. Besides, whatever new information you cram in will only displace all the important ideas you've spent weeks learning. Remember: You need to be alert and fully functional the day of the exam

Eat a healthy meal before the exam.

Whatever you do - do not go into the test room hungry! Eat a meal that is rich in protein and complex carbohydrates before the test. Avoid sugary foods; they will pump you up initially, but you might crash hard part way through the exam. While you do not want to consume a lot of unhealthy fat, you do need a little of the healthy stuff such as flaxseed or olive oil on a salad. Avoid fried foods; they tend to make you sleepy.

Have confidence in yourself!

Everyone experiences some anxiety when taking a test, but exhibiting a positive attitude banishes anxiety and fills you with the knowledge you really do know what you need to know. This is your opportunity to show how well prepared you are. Go for it!

Be sure to take everything you need.

Depending on the exam, you may be allowed to have a pen or pencil, calculator, dictionary or scratch paper with you. Have these gathered together along with your entrance paperwork and identification so that you are sure you have everything that is needed.

Do not chitchat with friends.

Let your friends know ahead of time that it is not anything personal, but you are going to ignore them in the test room! You need to find a seat away from doors and windows, one that has good lighting, and get comfortable. If other students are worried their anxiety could be detrimental to you; of course, you do not have to tell your friends that. If you are afraid they will be offended, tell them you are protecting them from your anxiety!

Common Test-Taking Mistakes

Taking a test is not much fun at best. When you take a test and make a stupid mistake that negatively affects your grade, it is natural to be very upset, especially when it is something that could have been easily avoided. So what are some of the common mistakes that are made on tests?

Do not fail to put your name on the test.

How could you possibly forget to put your name on a test? You would be amazed at how often that happens. Very often, tests without names are thrown out immediately, resulting in a failing grade.

Not following directions.

Directions are carefully worded. If you skim directions, it is very easy to miss key words or misinterpret what is being said. Nothing is worse than failing an examination simply because you could not be bothered with reading the instructions!

Marking the wrong multiple choice answer.

It is important to work at a steady pace, but that does not mean bolting through the questions. Be sure the answer you are marking is the one you mean to. If the bubble you need to fill in or the answer you need to circle is 'C', do not allow yourself to get distracted and select 'B' instead.

Answering a question twice.

Some multiple choice test questions have two very similar answers. If you are in too much of a hurry, you might select them both. Remember that only one answer is correct, so if you choose more than one, you have automatically failed that question.

Mishandling a difficult question.

We recommend skipping difficult questions and returning to them later, but beware! First of all, be certain that you do return to the question. Circling the entire passage or placing a large question mark beside it will help you spot it when you are reviewing your test. Secondly, if you are not careful to actually skip the question, you can mess yourself up badly. Imagine that a question is too difficult and you decide to save it for later. You read the next question, which you know the answer to, and you fill in that answer. You continue on to the end of the test then return to the difficult question only to discover you didn't actually skip it! Instead, you inserted the answer to the following question in the spot reserved for the harder one, thus throwing off the remainder of your test!

Incorrectly Transferring an answer from scratch paper.

This can happen easily if you are trying to hurry! Double check any answer you have figured out on scratch paper, and make sure what you have written on the test itself is an exact match!

Don't ignore the clock, and don't marry it, either.

In a timed examination many students lose track of the time and end up without sufficient time to complete the test. Remember to pace yourself! At the same time, though, do not allow yourself to become obsessed with how much time has elapsed, either.

Thinking too much.

Oftentimes, your first thought is your best thought. If you worry yourself into insecurity, your self-doubts can trick you into choosing an incorrect answer when your first impulse was the right one!

Be prepared.

Running out of ink and not having an extra pen or pencil is not an excuse for failing an exam! Have everything you need, and have extras. Bring tissue, an extra eraser, several sharpened pencils, batteries for electronic devices, and anything else you might need.

Conclusion

Congratulations! You have made it this far because you have applied yourself diligently to practicing for the exam and no doubt improved your potential score considerably! Passing your up-coming exam is a huge step in a journey that might be challenging at times but will be many times more rewarding and fulfilling. That is why being prepared is so important.

Study then Practice and then Succeed!

Good Luck!

Thanks!

If you enjoyed this book and would like to order additional copies for yourself or for friends, please check with your local bookstore, favorite online bookseller or visit www.test-preparation.ca and place your order directly with the publisher.

Feedback to the author may be sent by email to feedback@test-preparation.ca

Visit Us Online

Taking a test? We can help!

Complete study guides, practice test
test questions, study tips and more:

www.test-preparation.ca

Endnotes

Reading comprehension passages where noted below is used under the Creative Commons Attribution-Share-Alike 3.0 License. For details visit,

http://en.wikipedia.org/wiki/Wikipedia:Text_of_Creative_Commons_Attribution-ShareAlike_3.0_Unported_License

[1] What is Free Range Chicken In *Answers.com*. Retrieved Feb 14, 2009, from http://wiki.answers.com/Q/What_is_free-range_chicken.

[2] Grizzly Bear. In *Wikipedia*. Retrieved Feb 14, 2009, from http://en.wikipedia.org/wiki/Grizzly_Bear.

[3] Grizzly Polar Bear Hybrid. In *Wikipedia*. Retrieved Feb 14, 2009, from http://en.wikipedia.org/wiki/Grizzly%E2%80%93polar_bear_hybrid.

[4] Peafowl. In *Wikipedia*. Retrieved Feb 14, 2009, from en.wikipedia.org/wiki/Peafowl.

[5] Smallpox. In *Wikipedia*. Retrieved Feb 14, 2009, from http://en.wikipedia.org/wiki/Smallpox.

[6] Lightning. In *Wikipedia*. Retrieved Feb 14, 2009, from http://en.wikipedia.org/wiki/Lightning.

[7] Venus. In *Wikipedia*. Retrieved Feb 14, 2009, from http://en.wikipedia.org/wiki/Venus.

[8] Weather. In *Wikipedia*. Retrieved Feb 14, 2009, from http://en.wikipedia.org/wiki/Weather.

[9] Ebola Virus. In *Wikipedia*. Retrieved May 9, 2012, from en.wikipedia.org/wiki/Ebola_virus_disease.

[10] Megabat. In *Wikipedia*. Retrieved May 2012, from http://en.wikipedia.org/wiki/Megabat

[11] List of Greek and Latin Roots in English. In *Wikipedia*. Retrieved Feb 14, 2009, from http://en.wikipedia.org/wiki/List_of_Greek_and_Latin_roots_in_English.

[12] *Wiktionary*. Retrieved Feb 14, 2009, from http://en.wiktionary.org/wiki/.

CPSIA information can be obtained at www.ICGtesting.com
Printed in the USA
LVOW01s0420040714

392902LV00003B/3/P